HEBREWS

for

EVERYONE

HEBREWS

for

EVERYONE

TOM
WRIGHT

Knox Press

First published in Great Britain in 2003 by
Society for Promoting Christian Knowledge
Holy Trinity Church
Marylebone Road
London NW1 4DU

This second edition copublished in 2004 by the Society for Promoting
Christian Knowledge, London, and Westminster John Knox Press, 100
Witherspoon Street, Louisville, KY 40202.

04 05 06 07 08 09 10 11 12 13 — 10 9 8 7 6 5 4 3 2

British Library Cataloguing-in-Publication Data
A catalogue record for this book is available from the British Library.

ISBN: 0-281-05307-3 (U.K. edition)

United States Library of Congress Cataloging-in-Publication Data is
on file at the Library of Congress, Washington, D.C.

ISBN: 0-664-22793-7 (U.S. edition)

Typeset by Pioneer Associates, Perthshire
Printed in Great Britain at
Ashford Colour Press

CONTENTS

For
Robert and Leah
friends, neighbours, companions on the way

INTRODUCTION

On the very first occasion when someone stood up in public to tell people about Jesus, he made it very clear: this message is for *everyone*.

It was a great day – sometimes called the birthday of the church. The great wind of God's spirit had swept through Jesus' followers and filled them with a new joy and a sense of God's presence and power. Their leader, Peter, who only a few weeks before had been crying like a baby because he'd lied and cursed and denied even knowing Jesus, found himself on his feet explaining to a huge crowd that something had happened which had changed the world for ever. What God had done for him, Peter, he was beginning to do for the whole world: new life, forgiveness, new hope and power were opening up like spring flowers after a long winter. A new age had begun in which the living God was going to do new things in the world – beginning then and there with the individuals who were listening to him. 'This promise is for *you*,' he said, 'and for your children, and for everyone who is far away' (Acts 2.39). It wasn't just for the person standing next to you. It was for everyone.

Within a remarkably short time this came true to such an extent that the young movement spread throughout much of the known world. And one way in which the *everyone* promise worked out was through the writings of the early Christian leaders. These short works – mostly letters and stories about Jesus – were widely circulated and eagerly read. They were never intended for either a religious or intellectual elite. From the very beginning they were meant for everyone.

That is as true today as it was then. Of course, it matters that some people give time and care to the historical evidence, the meaning of the original words (the early Christians wrote in Greek), and the exact and particular force of what different writers were saying about God, Jesus, the world and themselves. This series is based quite closely on that sort of work. But the point of it all is that the message can get out to everyone, especially to people who wouldn't normally read a book with footnotes and Greek words in it. That's the sort of person for whom these books are written. And that's why there's a glossary, in the back, of the key words that you can't really get along without, with a simple description of what they mean. Whenever you see a word in **bold type** in the text, you can go to the back and remind yourself what's going on.

There are of course many translations of the New Testament available today. The one I offer here is designed for the same kind of reader: one who mightn't necessarily understand the more formal, sometimes even ponderous, tones of some of the standard ones. I have tried, naturally, to keep as close to the original as I can. But my main aim has been to be sure that the words can speak not just to some people, but to everyone.

The letter to the Hebrews is one of the most bracing and challenging writings in the New Testament. People often find it a bit difficult, because it uses ideas that are strange to us. But, like meeting a new friend, we will find as we get to know it that it is full of interest and delight, with a powerful message that comes home to today's and tomorrow's church as much as it did to yesterday's. So here it is: Hebrews for everyone!

Tom Wright

HEBREWS 1.1–5

God's One and Only Son

¹In many ways and by many means God spoke in ancient times to our ancestors through the prophets; ²but at the end of these days he spoke to us in a son.

> He appointed this son to be heir of all things;
> through him, in addition, he created the worlds.
> ³He is the shining reflection of God's own glory,
> the precise expression of his own very being;
> he sustains all things through his powerful word.
> He accomplished the cleansing needed for sins,
> and sat down at the right of the Majesty Supreme.
> ⁴See how much greater he is than the angels:
> the name he was granted is finer than theirs.

> ⁵For to which angel did God ever say, 'You are my son, today I became your father'? Or, again, 'I will be his father, and he will be my son'?

I had an email this morning from an old friend in another part of the world. He had heard that my daughter was getting married, and in congratulating me he brought me up to date on the progress of his own daughter. Now in her teens, she was wearing seven earrings, bright purple hair, and rings in her lip and navel as well. He told me all this as though seeking my sympathy for his plight, but underneath that I heard a very different note: pride and delight. I well remembered my friend's own teenage years: a typical rebel, with long hair, loud music, a cigarette hanging from his lip . . . clearly his daughter was (as we say) a chip off the old block. Looking at her, he could see his own true self. His character – or one aspect of it, at least – was shining out of her.

This is a cheerful and low-grade example of the sublime

and exalted point which the letter to the Hebrews offers as its opening description of God and his only son. The son is 'the shining reflection of God's own glory'; he is 'the precise expression of God's own very being'. He is, dare we say, not just a chip off the old block – as though there might be many such people, perfectly reflecting God's own inner being – but the unique son. Look at him, and it's like looking in a mirror at God himself. His character is exactly reproduced, plain to see.

Actually, the word used for 'precise expression' here is the Greek word *character*, the origin of our apparently identical English word. But this is an interesting word in both Greek and in English. When we talk about the 'characters' in a play, and when we talk about the 'characters' of an alphabet (the Hebrew 'characters', say, or the Japanese), what have the two got in common? Where does the idea begin?

At the bottom of it all, in the ancient world, lies the idea of engraving, or of stamping soft or hot metal with a pattern which the metal will then continue to bear. Though the ancient world didn't have printing presses such as we have had since William Caxton in the fifteenth century, it had early equivalents that were used, particularly, for making coins. The emperor would employ an engraver who carved the royal portrait, and suitable words or abbreviations, on a stamp, or die, made of hard metal. The engraver used the stamp to make a coin, so that the coin gave the *exact impression*, or indeed expression, of what was on the stamp.

The word *character* in ancient Greek was widely used to mean just that: the accurate impression left by the stamp on the coin. From there it came to mean both the individual letters that could be produced by this method (hence the 'characters' of a language) and the 'character', in the broader sense, of a person or thing: the sort of person, the 'type' if you like (think about that word, too). And this is what our writer is saying about Jesus. It is as though the exact imprint of the father's very nature and glory has been precisely reproduced in the soft metal of the son's human nature. Now it is there for all the world to see.

Stay with the image of the emperor and his engraver a moment longer, and think about the opening two verses of this remarkable letter. Supposing the emperor had been wanting for a long time to tell his subjects who he was, to give them a good idea of his character. And supposing the metal stamp, or die, hadn't been invented yet. The emperor would only be able to send out drawings or sketches, which might tell people something but wouldn't give them the full picture. Then, at last, the reality: hard metal on soft, original picture exactly reproduced. Yes, says the writer: God had for a long time been sending advance sketches of himself to his people, but now he's given us his exact portrait.

With this idea, written as a grand and rather formal opening to the letter, the writer invites us to look at the whole sweep of biblical history and see it coming to a climax in Jesus. (Unlike the letters of Paul, this one doesn't tell us who it's from or who it's intended for, which is frustrating at one level but shouldn't spoil our enjoyment of its marvellous and rich thought.) Look back at the great prophets: Abraham, Moses, Samuel, Elijah, and then of course the writing prophets like Isaiah, Jeremiah and the rest. Our author would have included David in the list as well, as we can see from the way he quotes the Psalms.

This opening sentence isn't just a rhetorical flourish. It tells us clearly how the argument of the whole letter is going to run. Again and again we start with a passage from the Old Testament, and the writer shows us how it points forwards to something yet to come. Again and again the 'something' it points forwards to turns out to be Jesus – Jesus, as in this passage, as God's unique son, the one who has dealt with sins fully and finally, the one who now rules at God's right hand, the one to whom even angels bow in submission.

The next passage will develop this last point more fully. But we should notice, before we go any further, that the passages our writer quotes in verse 5 are two of the Old Testament passages the early Christians used most frequently when they were struggling to say what had to be said about Jesus. Psalm 2.7 and 2 Samuel 7.14 both speak of the **Messiah**, the ultimate **son of David**, as God's own special son. Like all the early Christians, the writer of this letter begins his thinking with the belief that Jesus was and is the Messiah, Israel's true king. Everything else follows from that.

So, though we don't know who the author of this letter was, we know something even more important about him. Right from the start, he has his eyes fixed on Jesus; at the end of the letter, when he draws everything together, he urges us to have our eyes fixed on him, too (12.2; 13.8). Are you ready for the challenge?

HEBREWS 1.6–14

The Messiah Is Superior to Angels

⁶Again, when God brings the firstborn son into the world, he says,

Let all God's angels worship him.

⁷In relation to the angels, this is what it says:

God makes his angels spirits, and his servants flames of fire.

⁸In relation to the son, however, it says,

Your throne, O God, is for ever and ever;
the sceptre of uprightness is the sceptre of your kingdom;
[9]you loved justice and hated lawlessness,
therefore God, your God, anointed you with the oil of
    gladness,
as superior to your comrades.

[10]And, again:

You established the earth, O Lord, from the beginning;
and the heavens are the works of your hands;
[11]they will be destroyed, but you will remain;
all of them will grow old like clothing,
[12]you will roll them up like a cloak,
and they will be changed like clothing.
But you are the same, and your years will never give out.

[13]But to which of the angels did God ever say,

Sit at my right hand,
until I make your enemies a stool for your feet?

[14]Must we not say, then, that they are all servant spirits, sent to act on behalf of those who are to inherit salvation?

It was Christmas again, and we spent what seemed like a very long time not just buying presents but wrapping them up. Half the fun of Christmas morning, after all, is the exciting packages in glittering wrapping, with ribbons and bows, all telling you something about how wonderful the present itself will be.

But that Christmas one of the children was so excited by the wrapping, and inside the wrapping the beautiful box, that she almost ignored the present itself. Indeed, though she seemed pleased in a way with the present, later that day we found her behind an armchair playing with ... the box. She was using it as a tiny dolls' house for some of her smaller toys. It worked so well, and was after all very pretty. She had laid out the wrapping paper around it, to be a kind of stage set, a backcloth, for the game she was playing. The fact that I can't now remember what was in the box itself – the real present – makes the point.

Hebrews is anxious that the people it's written to shouldn't make that mistake. They are Jewish Christians, as indeed all the very earliest Christians were; but this letter seems to be written not in the very earliest period, but perhaps some time between AD 50 and AD 70, possibly even after that. By that time, some Jewish Christians had got quite used to being part of a family that included **Gentiles**. They had accepted that God's purposes, after long years of preparation, had now been fully unveiled. The wrapping had come off the present; and the present was Jesus himself, God's own, unique son, sent to fulfil everything the **law** and the prophets had spoken of. They could now move on from the earlier stages of God's purpose and gladly live out the new one which had dawned.

But for many other Jewish Christians things weren't so easy. Lots of their family members, and friends and neighbours too, hadn't accepted that Jesus was the **Messiah**, and regarded them as dangerously misguided and disloyal to all that God had said earlier on. All sorts of pressure would be put on them to try to make them go back to where they'd been before, to abandon this new-found movement with its strange claims and to take up again a position of living under God's law, the law given through Moses. The law was such a magnificent thing; why would you want anything else? After all, it wasn't just given by God, though that would be important enough. It came in splendid wrapping: it was given to Moses (so Jewish tradition declared) by angels ...

This is why the long argument of Hebrews – an argument designed to show that you can't go back to an earlier stage of God's purposes, but must instead go forwards, must press on eagerly from within the new stage to the one that is yet to come – begins with a demonstration, from the Jewish scriptures themselves, that the Messiah was always intended by God to be superior to the angels, and hence (as we discover in the next two chapters) superior to the law that they brought. The law wasn't fixed for all time, as many Jews thought then and still think today; it was part of God's preparation, part of the brilliant and beautiful wrapping in which the ultimate present, God's gift of his own self in the person of the son, would be contained. This is where the letter is warning against the mistake of playing with the wrapping instead of with the present itself.

There are three things in particular which Hebrews wants to say about the way in which the Messiah is superior to the angels, each of which anticipates fuller statements later on in the letter. After the opening in verse 6, when the writer quotes Psalm 97.7 to show that God intends the angels to worship the son, he quotes three more passages about the Messiah, to contrast him with the angels who, according to Psalm 104.4, quoted in verse 7, are servants of God rather than living embodiments of him.

First, in verses 8 and 9, the letter quotes Psalm 45.6–7. This is a breathtaking passage, because it addresses the king (the whole Psalm is about the king) as if he can be called 'God'. It speaks of the king, in this godlike way, as exercising a sovereign rule through which, as many passages said should be the case, uprightness, justice and the rule of true law are put into effect in the world. One of the great themes about God's future purposes throughout the Bible is that God longs for real justice. We who, through our newspapers and television, are all too aware that injustice and wickedness flourish all over the place could do worse than reflect on this promise. Indeed, God's aim of forgiving the sins of his people, about which this letter has so much to say, is all part of the larger aim, to create a world in which evil has at last no place. And the point of the Psalm, as Hebrews quotes it here, is that all this is to happen, not through angels (they are just assistants in the process), but through the true anointed king, the Messiah.

The second passage comes from Psalm 102.25–27 and picks up on the 'for ever and ever' in the previous quotation. There is coming a time, says the Psalm, when the present world, earth and **heaven** alike, will be rolled up like a scroll, and new heavens and a new earth will take their place. Hebrews returns to this theme at the end of chapter 12, and much of the letter from here to there is to be understood within this framework. God's preparatory purposes through the law and the prophets have reached their climax in the Messiah; and the Messiah himself will be the one who will see God's plan of salvation and justice through to the ultimate 'new age', the '**age to come**', the time of renewed heavens and earth. He is the same, yesterday, today and for ever (13.8); the angels were preparing the way, but he is the one whose life, and saving rule, will last to all eternity (see particularly chapter 7).

The third, shorter passage comes from Psalm 110, one of the passages which was widely used in early Christianity to interpret the meaning of Jesus' messiahship. Hebrews, too, will come back to it several times more. It speaks of the enthronement of God's true king at God's right hand, and of the sovereign rule which he will exercise until everything that thwarts his purpose of justice and salvation will be defeated. Once again, nothing like this is ever said about angels; they, Hebrews concludes, are simply servants, with a job to do within God's purposes. Once you see who the son really is, and the role he was always intended to play in God's plan, you won't want to go back to anything or anyone less.

Not many readers today, perhaps, will be tempted to abandon Christianity in favour of some form of Judaism – though it is important for us to understand why that was such an obvious pressure in the early days. But many today, including many in the churches, seem dissatisfied with what they have, and are eager to expand their spiritual horizons (as they might see it) to include angels, saints and other interesting distractions. Let this letter serve as a warning, and an encouragement. Don't start playing with the wrapping instead of the true present. Pay closer attention to who Jesus really is; to the role he played, and still plays, in God's plan; and to the life of worship and service to which he, and he alone, calls each one of us.

HEBREWS 2.1–4

Don't Neglect God's Salvation!

¹So, then, we must pay all the closer attention to what we heard, in case we drift away from it. ²You see, if the word which was spoken through angels was reliable, with appropriate punishment every time anyone broke it or disobeyed it, ³how shall we escape if we ignore a rescue as great as this? It started by being declared through the Lord, and it was confirmed to us by those who heard him; ⁴and God bore witness as well, along with them, in signs and wonders and many different types of powerful deeds, and by the holy spirit, distributed in accordance with his will.

A well-known story imagines a devout Christian stuck on a ledge halfway down a cliff. Hundreds of feet below, the sea rages around jagged rocks. Above him is a sheer, unclimbable wall of rock.

He prays fervently for God to rescue him. Suddenly, a huge eagle appears and invites him to climb on its back. He refuses. A little while later, a helicopter comes by, but he waves it away. Then a light aircraft circles around, offering to drop a rope ladder. Again he refuses it. He continues to pray, 'Lord, why don't you rescue me!' And God answers, 'I sent you a bird, a helicopter and a ladder; why didn't you use them?'

It's a silly story, of course, but it makes several important points. God does indeed answer prayer, but not always in the way we expect. God frequently acts *through* what seem like 'natural', or random, events. If we wait for a bolt from the blue to guide us, heal us or save us, we may miss the apparently 'ordinary' means that God will use – a map to guide us, a doctor to heal us, a helicopter to rescue us. And (the point Hebrews wants to get across in this passage) we will look very stupid if we ignore the very thing God is doing for us on the grounds that it isn't what we had expected or perhaps wanted.

In fact, the letter offers a sequence which looks for a moment not unlike the story. God has already sent the **law** through angels; look what happens if people ignore *that*. Now: what will happen if they refuse to listen to something even more important and powerful? God may have to conclude that they really aren't interested in being rescued, in being saved from the sin and injustice which rages around them like an angry sea, and which not only threatens to engulf us from the outside but which we discover, to our horror, inside us as well. That's why, in this passage and frequently later on, Hebrews insists not just that Christians must stick with what they've got, rather than abandoning it, but also that they must pay *closer* attention, must go deeper into the truth and **life** which is theirs because they belong to the **Messiah**.

The picture Hebrews uses in the first verse, indeed, may be echoing the idea of a dangerous sea: 'in case we drift away from' what we heard. Imagine being in a little motorboat, some way out from shore, needing to find your way along the coast to the right harbour. You need to keep the engine running and a firm hand on the tiller. If you don't, there is no guarantee that you will drift in the right direction, and every probability that you will drift in the wrong one – perhaps onto a rocky shore, or out to the wild ocean where you can't see land any more. This is a warning many Christians need, perhaps especially those who have grown up in a Christian family or as part of a regular church community. It's all too easy to suppose that we can take the pressure off, and allow other people to do the praying, the thinking, the serious business; we'll go along for the ride, we'll stop putting so much effort into it, we'll go with the flow. The problem is that if we haven't got our own motor running, and our own hand on our own tiller, we may drift further and further away without realizing it.

Or, worse perhaps, we may provide a 'drag' on the others. A small boy I once knew was out shopping with his mother, who was pushing his younger sister in a pushchair. As he got tired and bored, he held on to the pushchair himself, but instead of using his own efforts to walk he was hanging back, so that his mother (as she eventually and crossly realized) was drag-ging him along as well as pushing the baby and carrying the shopping. Often in church life there are people who have that effect on a congregation or a fellowship; often it's only some distance down the road when the rest realize what's going on. Each of us needs to ask ourselves from time to time whether we are the drifting type, or whether we are going forward, day by day and year by year, paying closer attention to the **message**, not assuming we know it all and can coast along from here on.

The central contrast in this passage, obviously, is between

the law of Moses, given through angels, carrying warnings and penalty clauses for those who disobeyed it, and the message concerning Jesus. Modern Western Christians have often seen this contrast in terms of the law as a threatening thing and the **gospel** of Jesus as a soothing, comforting, healing thing. There's much truth in that, but if we forget the other side of it we make the gospel a mere cosy blanket instead of the bracing, challenging, life-changing thing it really is. If the king, the president, the emperor, the prime minister, or whoever is important in your country, sent you a message by a special messenger, you would pay attention, wouldn't you? But, if he turned up in person to see you, you wouldn't just pay attention; you would feel your world was turning upside down. Well, the law was a message from the one true God, sent through the special messengers (the angels). But in the message of the gospel the King himself has come to speak to us directly. What will happen if we say we're too busy, we can't be bothered to come and speak to him, we're reading a nice book and can't tear ourselves away just now?

The writer then offers clear evidence, in case anyone should question him, that the coming of Jesus, and the message which came to them from him, really *was* a visit from the King in person. Jesus himself had declared the **good news** of God's **kingdom**; those who heard him confirmed that it had indeed been so (the way Hebrews says this implies strongly that the writer was not himself a **disciple** during Jesus' earthly ministry). Then, equally important, God himself bore witness to it: when the message was preached, things happened – signs, wonders, mighty deeds, presumably often of healing but perhaps other things too, sudden conversions, the transformation of families, synagogue communities, villages.

In particular, when people believed the message, they discovered a strange new energy inside themselves – a warm, disturbing, personal presence which enabled them to do new things, which put new ideas into their heads, which motivated and energized them to become different people from the inside out. The earliest Christians knew what to call this personal presence inside them: it was God's **holy spirit**, the gift of God's own presence and self, not just in Jesus, important though that was and is, but living within them. Hebrews doesn't often refer to the holy spirit dwelling in people; but this passage, and one or two others, show that the writer takes it for granted.

What evidence is there in your own life, and in your church, that the gospel message of Jesus is true and powerful? If you find that question difficult to answer, could it be because you or your church have begun to drift, ignoring the royal message to which you should be paying closer attention?

HEBREWS 2.5–9

Jesus as the Truly Human Being

⁵You see, God didn't place the world to come (which is what I'm writing about) under the control of angels. ⁶Someone has spoken of it somewhere in these terms:

What are humans, that you should remember them?
What is the son of man, that you should take thought for
    him?
⁷You made him a little lower than the angels,
You crowned him with glory and honour,
⁸And you placed everything under his feet.

When it speaks of everything being subjected to him, it leaves nothing that is not subjected to him. As things are at present, we don't see everything subjected to him. ⁹What we do see is the one who was, for a little while, made lower than the angels – that is, Jesus – crowned with glory and honour because of the suffering of death, so that by God's grace he might taste death on behalf of everyone.

One of the most dramatic stories in the Old Testament concerns the royal succession. King David was very old, and everybody knew he couldn't last much longer. He had a great many sons and daughters. One of his sons, Adonijah, got together with the head of the army and one of the senior priests and had himself proclaimed as king without David knowing. But David had promised his wife Bathsheba that her son, Solomon, would be king; and, when David heard what had happened, he had Zadok the **priest** and Nathan the prophet anoint Solomon king instead. (You can read the whole story in the first two chapters of 1 Kings.) Everything turned on the question: who did the king intend to rule in the kingdom that was to come?

That's the question that Hebrews now faces – only, instead of a **kingdom** to be ruled by a new king after the old one had died, it's all about the new world that is yet to be, and the way in which God intends that this coming world should be ruled. As verse 5 says, 'the world to come' is the main subject both of this passage and of the whole letter; that's why 'hope' is such a powerful theme throughout the entire book. And the thrust of a good deal of the argument is that, in Jesus the **Messiah**, this hope has burst into the world already, bringing sure signs of the new world that will eventually come to be.

The present passage moves through three stages to make this point. The first, continuing the theme of the previous two passages, is that God always intended his unique son to be superior to the angels, even to the angels through whom the Jewish **law** had been given. This time, though, he speaks of this superiority in terms of the *future role* that has been

14

marked out for the son. In the coming world, God intends that the original order of creation should finally be realized: the world is to be ruled, wisely and creatively, by human beings who themselves live in trusting obedience to God himself. In Genesis 1 and 2, Adam and Eve are given charge of the garden and the animals. This role, though corrupted in all sorts of ways through the 'fall' in Genesis 3, is reaffirmed in Psalm 8, from which Hebrews now quotes. What are human beings? asks the Psalm. Why does God treat them in such a special way, when they are so obviously small and insignificant in terms of the wider creation? The answer is mysterious and powerful: humans seem at the moment to be lower than the angels, a lesser order of beings, but God intends that they should become the world's true governors. That's what being 'crowned with glory and honour' means.

The passage, though, has an extra twist. The word for 'humans' in verse 6 is singular, 'a human being'. In the next line, the phrase '**son of man**', which to a Jewish reader could simply mean 'a typical human being', could also, to someone who knew either the book of Daniel or the teaching of Jesus, mean 'the Messiah' – highlighting the fact that the Messiah is now to be seen as the true, typical, authentic and representative human being. This is what Hebrews has in mind, as we can see from the way in which the last line of the quotation, about God placing everything under his feet, picks up the passage from Psalm 110 quoted in 1.13 ('sit at my right hand, until I make your enemies a stool for your feet'). Just like Paul in 1 Corinthians 15.20–28, Hebrews brings together these texts about the Messiah and about the Truly Human One in order to speak both of the *future* role of Jesus in God's new creation and of his *present* position, already exalted as Lord. The point which Hebrews adds, which Paul doesn't need for his argument, is that, according to Psalm 8, this means that the

Messiah is superior to the angels. This important part of his argument is now complete.

The second stage of this passage is the reflection, which we've already begun to notice, on how Jesus has already attained the status which God marked out for humans in general. Here we meet a point which we shall discover to be typical of the way Hebrews understands the Old Testament. The Psalm speaks of humankind in general as set in authority over the world, with 'everything subjected to him'. But, says Hebrews, this clearly hasn't happened yet. Humans are not ruling the world, bringing God's order and justice to bear on the whole of creation. Everything is still in a state of semi-chaos. How then can this Psalm be taken seriously?

The answer is that it *has* happened – in the case of Jesus. He is the representative of the human race. His exaltation as Lord, after his earthly ministry, suffering and death (in which he was indeed 'lower than the angels') has placed him in the role marked out from the beginning for the human race. He has gone ahead of the rest of us into God's future, the future in which order and justice – saving order, healing justice – will come to the world. The exaltation of Jesus, and the fact that we who follow him can celebrate that and live in the light of it, is one of the major themes of the whole book.

But how can something that's happened to Jesus, all by himself, be relevant for the rest of us? This brings us to the third stage of the passage, which will presently be developed further. Jesus is the *representative* of his people. In a parliamentary democracy, voters in each area elect someone to *represent* them in the central councils of state. They can't all be there themselves (in the way that all citizens could be present, and could speak and vote, in the small city of ancient Athens, the birthplace of democracy); so they find an appropriate way of appointing someone who is there *on their behalf*, carrying their hopes and fears, their needs and aspirations, in his or her own person. Thus, because the representative is there and they are not, he or she also acts as their *substitute*, doing for them what, for various reasons, they can't do for themselves.

Something like this is going on again and again in the New Testament when writers speak of Jesus both as Israel's Messiah and the world's true Lord. Jesus *represents* Israel, as its Messiah; and, since Israel was designed, in God's purpose, to be the people who would represent the whole world, he also represents that much larger community. As a result, he can stand in for them, doing for them what they couldn't do for themselves. Hebrews here puts it in a nutshell: in his suffering of death, Jesus has, by God's grace, been enabled 'to taste death on behalf of everyone'. A good deal of the letter will now be devoted to explaining how this comes about, and what it means. For the moment, we should simply celebrate the fact, which is central to all Christianity, that in Jesus God has already dealt with death on our behalf, and is already ruling the world as its rightful Lord.

HEBREWS 2.10–18

The Messiah and His Brothers and Sisters

[10]This is how it works out. Everything exists for the sake of God and because of him; and it was appropriate that, in bringing many children to glory, he should make perfect, through suffering, the one who leads the way to salvation. [11]For the one who makes others holy, and the ones who are made holy, all belong to a single family.

This is why he isn't ashamed to call them his brothers and sisters, [12]when he says,

I will announce your name to my brothers and sisters;
I will sing your praise in the middle of the assembly,

[13]and again,

I will place my trust in him,

and again,

Look, here I am, with the children God has given me.

[14]Since the children share in blood and flesh, he too shared in them, in just the same way, so that through death he might destroy the one who has the power of death, that is, the devil, [15]and set free the people who all their lives long were under the power of slavery because of the fear of death. [16]It's obvious, you see, that he isn't taking special thought for angels; he's taking special thought for Abraham's family. [17]That's why he had to be like his brothers and sisters in every way, so that he might become a merciful and trustworthy high priest in God's presence, to make atonement for the sins of the people. [18]He himself has suffered, you see, through being put to the test, and that's why he is able to help those who are being tested right now.

Some while ago there was a movie by the name of *A River Runs through It*. It told the story of two brothers growing up in the beautiful Montana countryside. The older one was quiet, studious, hard-working; he got a good job and became a respected man in the community. His tearaway younger brother was great fun, but was always getting into scrapes, pushing the boundaries of what was acceptable. He ended up associating with people who led him deeper and deeper into trouble, and was finally killed in a brawl. His older brother couldn't help him. They had grown too far apart.

It was a moving and tragic story, and the most tragic thing about it was this: the older son saw what was happening to his beloved younger brother, and there was nothing he could do about it. He couldn't reach him. He couldn't come to where he was and rescue him.

The point of the present passage is that Jesus, the older brother of a much larger family, could and did come to where his siblings were, wallowing in the land of sin and death. He identified with them, shared their fate, and thereby rescued them from it. Above all other passages in early Christian writings, this one speaks most fully about Jesus as the oldest brother, the firstborn, of a large family (Paul mentions this too, for instance in Romans 8.29, but doesn't develop it so thoroughly). It encourages us to see Jesus not as the kind of older brother whom we resent because he's always getting things right and being successful while we're always getting things wrong and failing, but as the kind of older brother who, without a trace of patronizing or looking down his nose at us, comes to find us where we are, out of sheer love and goodness of heart, and to help us out of the mess.

In sketching this picture, the author of Hebrews adds three more elements which give it its special colour. First, he sees Jesus as the pioneer: he is 'the one who leads the way'. Imagine an explorer cutting his way deep into the jungle. Nobody has been this way before; there are no paths, no trails, no signs that it's possible to go this way. Yet on he goes, forging his way through impossible terrain, until he reaches the goal. Once he's done that, others can follow.

Explorers do that sort of thing for various reasons: fame, fortune, sheer curiosity. Jesus did it out of love. The jungle was the whole world of suffering, pain, sin and death. Nobody had ever gone through there before and come out the other side. When he did it, he opened the way into God's new world, like our explorer coming through the jungle and out onto the sunlit uplands of the country beyond. And in leaving the jungle behind, and doing so on behalf of all those who will follow him, he gets rid of the world of sin and pollution that otherwise clings to the fallen human race. The biblical way of putting this is there in verse 11: he makes his people 'holy', that is, separated from sin and pollution, ready to enter the presence of the holy God.

The second element is that Jesus has done all this specifically through his death. In verse 12, Hebrews quotes from Psalm 22.22: 'I will declare your name to my brothers and sisters.' You might think that was simply a quotation to back up the point about Jesus bringing his siblings to a knowledge of God. But go back to Psalm 22 and read the first 21 verses. You will find that they describe, in horrendous detail, the suffering and death of the one who truly trusts in God and yet finds that he himself seems to be God-forsaken. 'My God, my God, why did you forsake me?' asks the Psalmist. On he goes, describing his torments and tortures. Finally, with the verse quoted here, the Psalm turns the corner. As a result of this suffering, salvation is accomplished, God's **kingdom** is coming, and a great multitude will give praise to God. Jesus' own vocation was made up, in part, of his deep understanding, and application to himself, of various Old Testament passages. Hebrews goes to those same passages to explain the meaning of his death.

In doing so, it picks up yet another vital and central biblical theme: the **Exodus** from Egypt. Israel had been enslaved to Pharaoh, and God went and rescued them. Now, declares this letter in verse 15, Jesus has set the slaves free – those who were enslaved under the fear of death. It's interesting that with all our modern thinking, technology and civilization we are still no nearer to getting rid of this fear than our ancestors were. The greatest philosophers of the last few hundred years have turned the question this way and that, but death remains the great mystery, the dark denial of the goodness and beauty that we know in our lives and in the world. And for many people this fact enslaves them in fear, a fear which Hebrews says comes through the **devil**, the one who is always opposed to God's good purposes in creation, and always tries to destroy that good world and to prevent the birth of the even better world that is to come. But God promised Abraham that he would have a great, worldwide family (verse 16); and it's this family that Jesus is concerned with, rescuing them from their slavery and pioneering the way to God's future world.

This leads to the third element, which introduces another major theme of the whole letter. In suffering and dying on behalf of his people, Jesus has become the true **high priest** who makes atonement for their sins. We shall have more to say about this later on, but note for the moment the assumption that Hebrews makes: that a true high priest, as set out in the Old Testament, should be on the one hand someone who is able to act as God's representative to his people, embodying God's mercy and reliability (verse 17), and on the other hand one who can fully sympathize with those to whom he ministers (verse 18). He is no distant older brother, unable to cross the gulf to rescue his siblings. He shared in flesh and blood, and even death itself (verse 14). There is nothing we face, today or tomorrow or the next day, in which Jesus cannot sympathize, help and rescue us, and through which he cannot forge a way to God's new world.

HEBREWS 3.1–6

Jesus and Moses

¹Well then, my brothers and sisters: you are God's holy ones, and you share the call from heaven. So think carefully about Jesus, the apostle and high priest of our confession of faith. ²He was faithful to the one who appointed him, just as Moses

was faithful in all God's house. [3]He deserves much more glory than Moses, you see, just as the one who builds a house deserves more glory than the house. [4]For every house is built by someone, but the one who builds all things is God. [5]And 'Moses was faithful, as a servant, in all his house', thereby bearing witness to the things that were yet to be spoken of; [6]but the Messiah is over God's house as a son. What is that house? It's us – those of us who hold on tightly to the free delight and confidence of our hope.

In the part of England where I grew up there were two main football clubs to support: Newcastle and Sunderland. Loyalty was, and remains, fierce: woe betide you if you found yourself wearing a black-and-white scarf (Newcastle) in the midst of a group of red-and-white supporters (Sunderland). I lived closer to Newcastle; I supported them, and still do.

But when I grew up and moved away from the area, I found that my loyalty to the entire region, over against the rest of the country, meant that I wanted both teams to do well. If Sunderland were playing against Manchester or Chelsea or Aston Villa, I wanted Sunderland to win. Only if I was forced to choose between Sunderland or Newcastle – when the teams actually played against each other, for instance – would I choose Newcastle, not out of a desire to see Sunderland do badly but because I supported Newcastle even more strongly than I supported Sunderland.

This helps me to understand the kind of argument Hebrews now offers about Jesus and Moses. The early Christians faced two equal and opposite pressures. On the one hand, traditional Judaism was quite clear that God had given Moses his **law**, and that this law was absolute and binding on God's people for all time. It was unalterable, inflexible, unchanging, uncompromising. If you took that line, then the best you could say about Jesus was that he was bringing some new insights into the keeping of the law; but Moses would remain the senior partner, and the law would continue to determine the shape of God's people. And that would mean that God's new age still hadn't arrived.

On the other hand, many early Christians were so excited to think that the new age had indeed arrived that they were eager to move as fast as they could in the opposite direction. They were with Jesus, therefore there was nothing good to say about Moses at all; nothing good to say about the law; nothing good to say about Israel BC . . . and hence they were in danger of cutting off the branch they were sitting on. They were, if you like, so keen on supporting Newcastle that they would be happy if Sunderland fell off the map.

Like Paul, the writer of Hebrews is determined to resist all pressures to move that way, just as he is equally clear that Jesus has indeed brought God's new age to birth, so that the law, the angels who gave it, and Moses who brought it to God's people, can't any longer have the last word. (At this point, of course, the parallel with football clubs breaks down.) Moses matters, says Hebrews, but Jesus matters even more; Moses was a true servant of God, but Jesus is God's son. You don't diminish Moses by making Jesus superior to him; you give him his rightful place, which is a place of honour even though it's not the supreme honour.

Now we see where the argument of the letter so far has been going. It's the first big point the writer wants his readers to grasp: that the purpose which God was working out through the long years of Israel's history, with Moses and the **Exodus** among the key founding people and moments, really has reached its goal with Jesus. This means that those who belong to Jesus, in the present, really are 'God's holy ones' (verse 1 – a title which would before this have been reserved for Jews who were strict in their adherence to the law of Moses, or for the angels themselves). They really do 'share the call from **heaven**', that is, from God.

This isn't simply a call to invite them to 'go to heaven'. As we shall see near the end of the letter, the writer envisages a whole new creation, just like the other New Testament writers do. Rather, it's a call *from* heaven, the call which comes through the risen and ascended Jesus rather than through the angels who gave the law. (See, too, 12.18–24.) He is, as verse 1 puts it, the '**apostle**', that is, the one 'sent from God'; and, as we saw before, he is the '**high priest**', who represents God to the people and the people to God. And the whole Christian movement, with Jesus as its apostle and high priest, can be summed up in a phrase typical of Hebrews, here at the end of verse 1: 'our confession of **faith**'. We need to spend a moment on this, because it comes again and again and we had better get it straight.

The word 'confession' today normally means 'telling someone you did something you shouldn't have'. It means 'owning up': 'Yes, officer, I was driving too fast'; 'Yes, I did break that cup when I was washing up'; 'Yes, I did slam the door when I left the room'. But the early Christians gave the word a wider meaning: 'telling people what's really true about your belief'. This means 'owning up', not to having done something wrong, but to believing in the Christian **message** and to belonging to the Christian movement: 'Yes, I do believe that Jesus is the **Messiah**, and that God raised him from the dead'; 'Yes, I do believe that all God's purposes and promises came true in Jesus'; 'Yes, I do belong to the family that Jesus regards as his brothers and sisters'.

'Confession' in this sense might get you into trouble, because in the first century, and in many parts of the world still today, believing and belonging like that is seen by authorities as a threat to their power and their system. But it's always been the Christian way, to 'own up' to being part of Jesus' extended family, whether that meets with a cheer or a snarl.

The main contrast between Moses and Jesus, then, is made with the picture of the servant and the son (verses 5 and 6). But Hebrews also speaks of the 'house', God's house, in which Moses worked as a servant but which Jesus owns as the son – the **son of the God** who builds the house. But what is this 'house'?

Most first-century Jews, faced with the idea of 'God's house', would think at once of the **Temple**. But Hebrews, again like Paul, and also like some other radical Jewish groups of the period, thought of the true 'house' not as a building of bricks and mortar but as a community of people.

The people who make up this house are described in verse 6 as a bold, confident family. There is no room here for the rather mealy-mouthed confession of faith one sometimes hears in the Western world ('some of us feel drawn to follow Jesus', implying that we might be wrong and that plenty of other people are just fine doing other things). Either you believe that God's new world has come to birth in Jesus and is there, waiting for us, as a solid and definite hope – which means you can be bold in living and acting on that basis, and can make sure and confident claims about it. Or you haven't really understood what Christianity is all about. This isn't a recipe for arrogance, using the **gospel** as an excuse for the kind of pride which covers up our own insecurities. Rather, it's a matter for cheerful celebration, knowing that the gospel and the hope it brings has nothing to do with our achievements, and everything to do with God's love and grace.

HEBREWS 3.7–13

Today's the Time to Listen!

⁷So listen to what the holy spirit says:

> Today, if you hear his voice,
> ⁸Don't make your hearts hard as in the great bitterness,
> Like the day in the desert when they faced the test,
> ⁹When your fathers put *me* to the test, and challenged me,
> And saw my works ¹⁰for forty years.
> And so I was angry with that generation,
> And said, 'They are always straying in their hearts,
> They do not know my ways.' ¹¹As I swore
> In my anger, 'They'll never enter my rest.'

¹²Take care, my dear family, that none of you should possess an evil and unbelieving heart, leading you to withdraw from the living God. ¹³But encourage one another every day, as long as it's called 'Today', so that none of you may become hardened by the deceitfulness of sin.

Some of the party had never seen snow before. One in particular, who had lived all his life in Kenya until coming to university in England, had read about it in books and seen pictures of it, and had tried to imagine what it was like. But the reality was quite different, and he was excited. As we walked and climbed up the steep side of the mountain that January day, he and the others had great fun making large footprints in the deepening snowdrifts, throwing snowballs at each other, and putting out their tongues to taste what the snow would be like as it swirled around us, soft and enticing. We couldn't see very far ahead, but we didn't mind. It was an adventure.

After a couple of hours of climbing, though, the mood

changed dramatically. The novelty had worn off. The temperature, which had been just below freezing when we set out, had dropped sharply, and there must have been at least fifteen degrees of frost. As we had climbed higher, the wind had increased and was now biting into our faces and anything else exposed (one or two of the party hadn't brought gloves, and were trying to pull their sleeves down over their hands). My Kenyan friend discovered something else he'd previously only read about: the pores of black people and white people are different in size, and he was getting colder than we were, and at a faster rate. People were lending him extra layers of warm clothing. And, as we used up energy, so enthusiasm levels began to fall as well. There were mumblings of discontent. At one point someone suggested that we should quit and turn back. Someone else suggested (a barbed shot at me, I think) that we shouldn't have set out at all in this weather. We could still be sitting by a cosy warm fire reading a nice book.

Fortunately, just at this point, we got to the crest of the mountain, where we came upon the remains of an old sheepfold. It provided enough shelter for all of us to get out of the wind and blowing snow, and we were able, not without difficulty because of frozen fingers, to get out the food and drink we'd brought with us. Soon everyone was feeling better; it's remarkable how food and mood go together. We equipped our Kenyan with still more woollen clothes and finished the walk in good style. Everyone afterwards agreed they'd had a good time.

That cycle – of enthusiastic beginnings, grumbling when things got tough, and then provision of enough to go on with – describes more or less the wanderings of the children of Israel in the wilderness after they had come out of Egypt. We can trace at this point in Hebrews something of the same narrative sequence; we've just been thinking about Moses and the giving of the **law**, and now we're thinking about the wilderness wanderings, the 40 years they all spent in the desert before, finally, they were allowed to enter the land they had been promised. During that time they went through what the writer of Psalm 95 calls 'the great bitterness', the time of testing, when the people faced the test of whether or not they were going to trust God to provide for them, and they in turn put God to the test by demanding signs of his presence and care.

Hebrews wants its readers to think of themselves as in some ways like that generation, walking through the wilderness on the way to God's promised future; and they mustn't make the mistakes that the Israelites did. But it's not just a matter of thinking back to that tiring journey and deciding to behave differently this time. It's more a matter of that journey being a preliminary stage in a longer story, and the early Christians finding themselves at the new stage of the same longer story. To make the point, the writer quotes this Psalm, 95.7–11. From here until halfway through the next chapter (4.10) he's going to be coming back to it again and again, so we had better get to know it.

The Psalm is a great call to worship and praise. It opens with a lively invitation to sing and make a joyful noise. It celebrates the fact that YHWH is a great God, the king of all possible gods. He is the rock of our salvation, the creator of **heaven** and earth; he is the shepherd and we are the sheep. Our response ought to be to fall down and worship him. But with verse 7 the mood changes. The Psalmist, writing many centuries after the **Exodus**, warns that a new day is dawning in which it will matter decisively whether or not the people who hear this call to worship obey it or not. God had warned the people in the wilderness that, if they grumbled and rebelled and put him to the test, they wouldn't be allowed to enter his 'rest' – in other words, to find their settled home in the promised land. In the same way, says the Psalmist, you now are facing a choice: either worship and serve this same God, or run the risk of missing out on the 'rest' which is promised to you in turn.

The challenge becomes more urgent with the word 'Today', the point in the Psalm at which the quotation begins, and the point to which Hebrews returns several times, both in this passage and later. Along with the other early Christians, the writer believed passionately that God had acted once for all in Jesus the **Messiah**, and that as a result the new day had dawned for which Israel had been waiting. They had been living in what you might call 'tomorrow mode' for long enough; now it was 'today mode', the moment when suddenly it was all happening. If only they would remember that, they would stay on track.

There is much more exploration of Psalm 95 to come in the following passages. But notice especially the application Hebrews makes at once, in verses 12 and 13. The writer is all too aware that within every Christian community, even in the first generation, there were some who were in danger of going along with the others for the sake of companionship, but whose hearts weren't really in it. They were like people coming on a snowy mountain walk because they were with friends, but who hadn't really thought about what clothes they would need or what food to bring. So, when things got difficult, their heart would fail them, because it had never really believed in the venture in the first place. Even two or three such people on a mountain walk, let alone in a Christian fellowship, can cast a real shadow over everything else. Nobody likes to have to drag along a grumbling companion when you should all be giving yourselves wholeheartedly to the task in hand.

It isn't just a matter of people who were never really signed up in the first place. There may be others who made a genuine beginning, but who need regular encouragement (verse 13).

There is such a thing as 'the deceitfulness of sin', and it's very powerful. You start by allowing yourself the apparent luxury of doing something small which you know you shouldn't but which you think doesn't matter. When it becomes a habit, you stop thinking it's wrong at all. If the question is raised, you are ready with rationalizations: everyone does it, this is the way the world is now, you mustn't be legalistic, no good being a killjoy. This creates a platform for the next move: here's something else which a while ago you would have shunned as certainly wrong, but it's quite like the thing you've got used to, so maybe . . . And before too long you're rationalizing that as well. And once the mind has been deceived, the habit will continue unchecked.

The main problem with which Hebrews is concerned, and with it the main deceit, is the question of whether or not we continue to follow and trust Jesus, or whether we will be content to drift, with our initial belief fading away to a memory, and our hope dissolving like the energy of the snowbound walkers. 'Maybe we should never have come; maybe this mountain doesn't have a summit anyway . . .'

HEBREWS 3.14–19

Hold on Tight!

[14]We share the life of the Messiah, you see, only if we keep a firm, tight grip on our original confidence, right through to the end. [15]That's what it means when it says, 'Today, if you hear his voice, don't make your hearts hard, as in the great bitterness.'

[16]Who was it, after all, who heard and then became bitter? It was all those who went out of Egypt under Moses, wasn't it? [17]And who was it that God was angry with for forty years? It was those who sinned, wasn't it – those whose bodies fell in

the desert? [18]And to whom did God swear that they would never enter his rest? Wasn't it the people who didn't believe? [19]So we can see that it was their unbelief that prevented them from entering.

Nobody wants to fall asleep while driving a car. But a remarkable number of people do it.

In the UK at least, there are now signs on the major roads that warn motorists of the danger of sleepy driving. 'Tiredness can kill,' they say. You'd think it would be obvious; fancy hurtling down the road at 70 miles an hour while being sound asleep. The newspapers have recently reported that the courts are going to impose much more severe penalties for people who have gone to sleep at the wheel and caused serious or fatal accidents.

But I know how it happens. Two or three times in my life I have found myself, of necessity, driving late at night after a long, tiring day. Even if you stop regularly and drink a lot of coffee, there comes a point when the whole body is sending signals to the brain, to the imagination, to the will, whispering louder and louder that it wouldn't matter if you just shut your eyes for a moment . . . it would only be for a minute or two . . . after all, the car's going along quite merrily just now, surely it can do without you just for a couple of seconds . . .

And of course if you give in at that moment you're in real danger, and so is everyone else anywhere near you on the road. But the point I'm making is that, while nobody gets into the car with the aim of falling asleep halfway to their destination, the physical effects of tiredness include the deceitful whispers that tell you it'll be all right really, nothing bad will happen, you might as well nod off for a minute. And when those whispers happen, one of the things you need is clear thinking. You need to recognize the state you're in, and take quick and decisive action.

Recognizing the state you're in spiritually and morally is something few Christian teachers have had anything to say about in recent years, at least in the parts of the church where I work. We have heard so much about 'following your own spiritual path', and 'continuing your own journey of **faith**', that we can easily get the impression that we should merely do whatever feels best at the time, and hope that it'll all work out somehow. Well, it may, but it may not. There are times in Christian living which correspond to those moments of sudden sleepiness in the car, times when for whatever reason there is a persuasive whisper in your ear telling you that you might as well take a break now, that it doesn't really matter if you give in to this temptation, that you don't need to make an effort in prayer or reading the Bible or taking thought and care for your neighbours or working for God's justice in the world. It all seems so much effort. It would be much easier to slack off for a bit . . .

When you find yourself thinking like that, you need to do the mental and spiritual equivalent of stopping the car, getting out, having a cup of coffee and doing some brisk physical exercise, or even get some proper rest (like going on a retreat – which is perhaps the equivalent of stopping at a wayside hotel for the night). And the point of the present passage, continuing the exposition of Psalm 95, is that we need this spiritual discipline all the way through our lives to the very end. As verse 14 insists, we need to keep a firm, tight grip on our original confidence. If we aren't quite as wide awake as we were when we set off, we need to take steps to get ourselves back into that condition. Otherwise, in spiritual language, our hearts will become hard and bitter (verse 15) – the spiritual equivalent of nodding off to sleep while driving.

Hebrews rams the point home with the three questions of verses 16, 17 and 18. Who was it who heard and became bitter?

It wasn't people who lived in the wilderness anyway, who knew nothing except a hard and difficult life and who could be expected to be grumpy about it. It was the children of Israel, who had come out of Egypt under Moses's leadership, and had seen everything God had done at the Red Sea, not to mention the powerful signs of judgment on Egypt before they had left. Don't think, in other words, that just because you had the best of intentions when you got into the car you won't feel sleepy some way down the road. Don't think it can't happen to you. It can. If you don't watch out, it will.

And who was it that God was angry with? It wasn't a different people, **Gentiles**, pagans, people outside the family God had chosen and called out of Egypt, a different people who weren't descended from Abraham, Isaac and Jacob. No: it was his own people, who had gone against his word, who heard what he said and did the opposite. Again, the writer is insisting: this warning isn't for the person standing next to you. It's for you. Yes, you.

And, finally, what matters is continuing to believe. Many of the people in the wilderness simply stopped believing that God was really with them, really leading them. Again and again they accused Moses of simply tricking them so that he could lead them where he wanted. When they came close to the promised land, early on in their wanderings, the spies who went to look over the land told the people what a dangerous and difficult place it was, so that they stopped believing in God's promises and instead believed a lie. That's the ever-present danger which faced Christians in the first century, and which faces us today as well. Once you stop believing either in the God who called you, rescued you and guides you, or in the future he has promised you, you may simply go round and round in the wilderness and never get anywhere. And – to go back to our sleepy driver once more – once you give in to the impulse, you will not only put yourself at risk. All the other people whose lives you touch will be in danger as well.

HEBREWS 4.1–10

Getting through to the Sabbath Rest

¹So we are bound to worry that some of you might seem to have missed out on God's promise of entering his rest, the promise which is still open before us. ²For we certainly had the good news announced to us, just as they did; but the word which they heard didn't do them any good, because they were not united in faith with those who heard it. ³For it is we who believe who enter, as it is written,

> As I swore in my anger,
> They will never enter my rest

– even though God's works had been complete since the foundation of the world. ⁴For it says this somewhere about the seventh day,

> And God rested on the seventh day from all his works,

⁵and again, in the present passage,

> They will never enter my rest.

⁶Therefore, since some failed to enter into it, and those who received the good news earlier on didn't enter because of unbelief, ⁷he once again appoints a day, 'Today', saying through David – after such a long interval of time! – in the words already quoted,

> Today, if you hear his voice,
> Don't harden your hearts.

[8]If Joshua had given them rest, you see, he wouldn't be speaking about another subsequent 'rest'. [9]Thus we conclude: there is still a future sabbath 'rest' for God's people. [10]Anyone who enters that 'rest' will take a rest from their works, as God did from his.

I once heard a story about a priest who was fond of riding his horse – too fond, it turned out, because he was always out riding when he should have been working in his parish. So, according to the story, he called his horse 'Sabbatical', so that when people asked where he was his wife could say, perfectly truthfully, that he was 'on Sabbatical'.

Among the many signs that the story is apocryphal is that clergy sabbaticals are a very recent invention, and have only become popular since horse-riding among clergy became a rare eccentricity; but it serves to remind us that in biblical theology there is a principle of 'one day in seven', or possibly 'one year in seven', or some variation on these, which is built into creation from the beginning. By the time of Jesus, the parts of the Mosaic **law** which dealt with **sabbath** observance had become such a tightly drawn legal system that people were forgetting their purpose, which was to help people by giving them rest, not to add burdens to them by forbidding things like healing. Jesus had to break through all that, as we see in the **gospels**. But nowhere does the New Testament deny that the principle set out in Genesis 1 remains important: a day of rest once a week, corresponding to God's day of rest at the end of creation.

In our present passage, though, the idea of God's rest on the seventh day of creation comes into its own in a different way. We have already seen that Hebrews is using Psalm 95 to talk about the 'rest' which the Israelites had been promised once they reached their destination. Now the writer links this with

God's own 'rest' at the end of creation, suggesting that, since God was warning that the people might not enter into 'his rest', that implied that the promise of the land was meant to function for them like the 'rest' which he had enjoyed after his six days of creative work.

The full force of the passage, though – and with it the thrust of this whole section of the letter – comes in verses 8 and 9. When the people did eventually reach the land, under the leadership of Joshua, they entered into the 'rest' which they had been promised. They could at last stop wandering – after forty years, not six days! – and enjoy the new period of settled life with all its opportunities to develop culture, agriculture, trades and occupations of all sorts, and build homes and communities. But now, says Hebrews, just think about it. That had already occurred – Joshua had already given them this 'rest' – a long time before David wrote Psalm 95. (This Psalm doesn't actually say that David wrote it, but most people in the first century believed he had written most of them, and, if he didn't, that means it was probably written after his time, which only makes the point all the more sharply.) So what on earth is David doing speaking of a *further* 'rest', so long after they had already attained the one they had been promised when they came out of Egypt?

Hebrews gives the answer, typical of several arguments in this letter: the only way to make sense of Psalm 95 is to see that it was pointing forwards, looking ahead to yet another 'rest' which, from the Psalmist's point of view, was still to come in the future. We are faced, then, with a sequence of three 'rests': God's own rest on the seventh day of creation; the 'rest' which Joshua gave the people when he brought them into the promised land; and the future 'rest' which the Psalm promised, and which, according to Hebrews, remains still as a promise looking into the future.

36

Nor do we have to search far to find out what that future and final 'rest' might be. In chapters 11 and 12 the vision of God's future opens out, as the writer lists all the heroes of **faith** from ancient times who, as in this Psalm, looked ahead to a new kind of land, a new sort of city, the city and land which are at present in God's own part of creation ('**heaven**'), and which will be brought to full reality after the present heaven and earth have been 'shaken' one more time (12.25–28).

As we sit back and gaze at this picture, here are two small but important details to notice within it. First, in verse 8, the writer mentions Joshua, the leader who took over after the death of Moses. It's almost the only time he is named in the whole New Testament (Acts 7.45 is the other instance). But the name 'Joshua', in both Greek and Hebrew, is the same as the name 'Jesus'. That's why, in some older translations, verse 8 says 'if Jesus had given them rest', causing confusion for many readers. But the letter is well aware of the parallel, as well as the difference, between Joshua and Jesus. Joshua gave the people their first 'rest'; Jesus of Nazareth, the **Messiah**, will give them their final 'rest'.

Second, according to verse 10, the final 'rest' will mean stopping work. There may be a hint here of something like Paul's strongly held point that what matters is not 'works', but 'faith'. It certainly is faith, that is, a trusting belief in God, that this writer wants to emphasize as his exposition of Psalm 95 comes to an end. The point may be that the 'rest' will always remain God's gift, not something we can ever construct for ourselves by hard work.

The writer is anxious (verse 1) that his readers may be in danger of missing out on the final 'rest', since they may fall into imitating those who, in the wilderness, refused to align themselves with those who did believe (verse 2). He stresses it again in verses 3 and 6: belief is what matters, so be sure you

37

really do believe! This will be the major theme of chapter 11 as well, where he gives some definitions of believing faith and, perhaps more important still, several classic examples of saints of old who believed despite apparently impossible odds.

That's what counts today as much as ever. Some Christians today live in long-established churches where everything is in danger of getting a bit sleepy; nobody can really believe it can be as good as it was in the old days (which are usually, of course, a romantic fiction). Other Christians live in churches which are struggling for survival within a hostile environment of religion or politics where the Christian gospel is felt as a threat. It's hard, then, to believe that the gospel really is the way through to God's new world. All of us face the challenge to trust God rather than to trust the way we feel or the things we see in front of us. All of us need to keep before our eyes the promise of God's eventual, and eternal, 'rest'.

HEBREWS 4.11–13
Danger! God's Word at Work

¹¹So, then, let's make every effort to enter that 'rest', so that nobody should trip and fall through the same pattern of unbelief. ¹²God's word is alive, you see! It's powerful, and it's sharper than any double-edged sword. It can pierce right in between soul and spirit, or joints and marrow; it can go straight to the point of what the human heart is thinking, or intends to do. ¹³No creature remains hidden before God. All are naked, laid bare before the eyes of the one to whom we must present an account.

I washed the kitchen knife, put it down for a moment and then picked it up to dry it. As I did so, I felt what seemed like a slight tickle at the end of one finger. I looked down, and to my surprise and alarm saw blood spurting out of a neat, straight cut across the end. I hadn't realized that our new kitchen knife had a double blade, and in picking it up – carefully, as I'd imagined – I had for a moment run my finger across the reverse side, which seemed to have been every bit as sharp as the main edge. The sharper a blade is, of course, the less you feel when you cut yourself. It had gone straight through skin and into flesh with no trouble at all.

That's the image Hebrews is using in verse 12 to describe the effect of God's word in someone's **life**. It's sharp enough to go straight in, almost without you realizing it. The difference is that the writer isn't talking about a carving knife, but a sword, a weapon that would not just cut into a finger but could very easily go right through your body, into heart, liver, kidneys or lungs. No escape.

What about protection, then? Any chance of body armour, to stop the blade from getting near your flesh? No. Nothing. Verse 13 is quite clear: when it comes to God and his **word**, there is nowhere to hide. Indeed, we shall one day have to make an account of our lives, our inner lives and outer lives alike, before God. Hebrews isn't a very relaxing book, is it?

No; but a very necessary one. What the author does *not* want to see happen is any of those to whom he is writing – which, by extension, includes you and me as we read his text today – coming to grief, literally as well as metaphorically, by the steady erosion of belief that results in rank *un*belief, which in turn will result in failing to enter the 'rest'. If it's relaxation you want, don't expect too much of it in the present Christian life; but remember that you are promised a real 'rest' at the end! The road to that 'rest' is labelled 'belief', 'holding on', 'keeping a firm grip on the confession of **faith**', and so on.

But what has the sharp, dangerous two-edged sword of God's word got to do with all this?

It's a bit too easy for us today to think that by 'God's word' a New Testament writer meant simply 'the Bible'. For a start, not all of it was even around then; we don't know when this letter was originally written, and it's quite likely that other New Testament books came later. We have no reason to suppose that the author of Hebrews even knew about the other books that were already written; and, though the writers of the New Testament clearly intended their work to be seen as authoritative for the church, and in that sense 'scripture', there is no evidence for a definite *collection* of early Christian works that were regarded in this way until well into the second century.

Did 'God's word' simply mean the *Old* Testament, the Jewish Bible, then? In a sense, yes. The point of the remark in verse 12 seems to be that the scriptural texts which Hebrews has been using, notably (in the last two chapters) Psalm 95, have an uncanny knack of going right to the heart of things, or more especially right to the heart of *people*. When people read them or hear them, they find themselves, as we say, 'opened right up', made aware not only of new truth coming in from the outside but, perhaps more worrying, of what was going on inside them, things they had managed to keep hidden even from themselves.

But the way the New Testament writers use the phrase 'God's word' suggests that they meant more (not less) than the Old Testament. They also meant the **message** which Jesus himself announced – that God's **kingdom** was coming to birth in and through his work – and then the message *about* Jesus and what he'd done, essentially the same message but from a new perspective. However, since the point of what Jesus had done was precisely that it fulfilled the prophecies of the Old Testament, which is after all what this letter is mostly about, we can put the two together quite easily. 'God's word' seems to mean 'the ancient scriptures, and the message about how they all came true in Jesus'.

So what is it exactly that God's word is supposed to do? And how can we respond to its challenge?

Well, part of the point of verses 12 and 13 is that it's going to do its work, and you can't escape! But clearly a lot of people *do* escape for the moment at least, presumably either by staying out of earshot of it – making sure they don't open a Bible too often, and don't listen to sermons or even general chatter about Jesus if they can help it – or firmly ignoring anything they do hear. But part of what this passage seems to be saying is that you can't escape *in the end*; that if you imagine you can slide along in unbelief and slip by unnoticed into the 'rest' that God has promised his faithful people, God's word will find you out, will pierce through and disclose what's really going on, the secret thoughts, plans and intentions that you make the real centre of your life. Everyone must sooner or later give an account of themselves. At that moment, if never before, all will be revealed.

But the thrust of the passage, though obviously intended as a warning, can also lead to a great encouragement. If this is going to happen sooner or later, you had much better get on with it. If you have a choice between letting the doctor examine you right away, uncomfortable though it may be, and waiting until he or she can do a post-mortem on you after it's too late, it's wise to go for the first. If you open yourself, day by day and week by week, to the message of scripture, its grand sweep and its small details, and allow the faithful preaching of Jesus and his achievement to enter your consciousness and soak down into your imagination and heart, then the admittedly uncomfortable work of God's word will be happening on a regular basis, showing you (as we say) where you really are, what's going on deep inside.

You may need help from someone else in this process. Just as the healing work of the early church didn't mean that

doctors became unnecessary, so the probing, searching, pene-
trating analysis of God's word doesn't mean that there isn't
still a job for psychotherapists and similar professionals. But
nor do they make the task of the word unnecessary. To spend
time, prayerfully and thoughtfully, with scripture and with
Jesus, the written and living **Word** of God, is to know that
gentle but powerful touch, like a very sharp and fine blade,
producing surprising and perhaps alarming results. But,
unlike my encounter with a new kitchen knife, with God's
word there are no accidents. God's word is alive, as verse 12
declares; and the purpose of the two-edged sword is always to
cleanse and heal.

HEBREWS 4.14—5.3
The Sympathetic High Priest

[14]Well, then, since we have a great high priest who has gone
right through the heavens, Jesus, God's son, let us hold on
firmly to our confession of faith. [15]For we don't have a high
priest who is unable to sympathize with our weaknesses, but
one who has been tempted in every way just as we are, yet
without sin. [16]Let us then come boldly to the throne of grace,
so that we may receive mercy, and may find grace to help us at
the moment when we need it.

[5.1]Every high priest, you see, is chosen from among human
beings, and is placed before God on their behalf, so that he can
offer gifts and sacrifices for sins. [2]He is able to sympathize
with people who don't know very much, or who wander off in
different directions, since he too has his own share of weakness. [3]That's why he has to offer sacrifices in relation to his
own sins as well as those of the people.

I have just finished reading a fascinating wartime diary, written
by an Anglican clergyman who was captured by the Germans

in 1940 and spent the next five years in various prison camps, ministering as best he could to the thousands of men who were ill-fed, badly housed and prone to despair. I have learned many things from the book, not least a reminder to be grateful that my own generation, though we have faced many other problems, have at least been spared that kind of experience.

As an appendix to the book, the author included a short essay, a character sketch of an Australian soldier who was in the same camp for a while. Tom Moore was in charge of the Australian barrack, which meant that he was responsible both to the German authorities for the state of the barrack and to the Australians for representing the interests of the men. To quote the writer, John H. King:

> The authorities expect him to see their displeasure when anything is wrong with the state of the barrack or the behaviour of the men. On the other hand, the men look to him to champion their rights and liberties, real and imagined. To carry out the job efficiently and to retain the confidence of both sides is a rare achievement . . . but Tom succeeded.

He spent most days going to and fro between Germans and Australians, and the other leading figures in the camp, making sure everything was sorted out despite the appalling conditions. He won universal respect.

This is the kind of intermediary role which Hebrews now describes in terms of the **high priest**hood which Jesus continues to hold. Of course, as with some of Jesus' own **parables**, not all the details fit: I'm not suggesting that God the father is like a hostile officer, or indeed that the church is like an army barrack in a prison camp. But the strong point to which we come, which opens the main central section of the letter, running from now to the end of chapter 7, is that Jesus has fulfilled the ancient promise of God that he would eventually send his people a great high priest who would do in perpetuity, and perfectly, what the regular priesthood symbolized but could only do in part, and imperfectly.

The promise itself, and the detailed exposition of it, will come shortly. But, by way of introduction, the writer pictures Jesus, like the young Australian officer, as the one who both belongs firmly on 'our side' of the picture and is completely at home, and able to represent us fully and appropriately, on God's side. He was, and remains, one of us, a truly human being who still remembers what it was like to be weak, to get sick, to be tempted over and over from every angle. (Don't make the mistake that some Christians have made, of imagining that Jesus, having become human in the incarnation, stopped being human after his death. One of the central beliefs of the early Christians, not least in this letter and those of Paul, is that Jesus remains fully and gloriously human, and that it is as a human being that he rules the world.) When he represents us before the father, he isn't looking down on us from a great height and being patronizing about those poor creatures down there who can't really do much for themselves. He can truly sympathize. He has been here. He knows exactly what it's like.

So where is he now, what's he doing and how does it affect us? Verse 14 says that he has 'gone right through the **heavens**'. Various ancient Jewish writings speak of different levels of 'the heavens'; Paul speaks in 2 Corinthians 12.2 of being caught up into 'the third heaven'. When Solomon built the **Temple**, he declared that 'heaven and the heaven of heavens cannot contain God' (1 Kings 8.27). Though different writers put it differently, the impression is that within 'heaven' (God's part

44

of the two-sided created order, as opposed to 'earth', the space-time cosmos we humans live in) there are layers, with God's own dwelling being the innermost one.

The point is that Jesus, having died and been raised from the dead, was then exalted, in the ascension, through all the different layers of 'the heavens', right to the very heart, to the throne of the father himself. He didn't, in other words, simply go to a convenient resting place in some spiritual sphere where he could remain, satisfied with having accomplished his earthly work. He went right to his father's inner courtroom, in order that by representing us there, by interceding for us with the father, he might continue to *implement* the work he had *accomplished* on earth. Once again, Paul says something similar, this time in Romans 8.34.

So when we come to pray to the heavenly father, we are not shouting across a great gulf. We are not trying to catch the attention of someone who has little or no concern for us. Verse 16 puts it like this: we are coming to 'the throne of grace' (that's a way of saying (a) that we're coming to the throne of God and (b) that we must now think of God as the God of grace), and we may and must come boldly and confidently. This isn't arrogance. Indeed, if we understand who Jesus is, what he's done and what he's still doing on our behalf, the real arrogance would be to refuse to accept his offer of standing before the father on our behalf, to imagine that we had to bypass him and try to do it all ourselves. What is on offer, for those who come to God through Jesus, is 'mercy and grace': mercy, to set us free from the sin and folly in which we would otherwise sink completely; grace, to strengthen us and set us on our feet for our own lives of service and witness.

The start of chapter 5 picks up the notion of the high priest and develops it further, preparing for the major statement of the theme which comes in the following passage. Many

Christians today in the various free church traditions don't often reflect on the nature of priesthood, since their view of Christian ministry is different. Indeed, one of the strengths of those traditions is to insist (along with the Catholic and Orthodox churches, at their best) that the Old Testament priesthood is precisely *not* continued in Christian ministry, but rather that it came to its climax, and in a sense its conclusion, in Jesus himself. All Christian ministry derives from that of Jesus, but cannot simply copy it. What he did, as this letter insists, was 'once for all'.

So what did the writer mean by priesthood, and how does this set him up for his portrait of Jesus?

He expounds the regular Jewish view, rooted in the ancient scriptures: the **priest**, and particularly the high priest, is there to be a bridge between the people and God. On the one hand, he has a liturgical and ceremonial role, offering gifts and **sacrifices**. These are not designed to twist God's arm, as though what humans do could put God in their debt, but to thank God for creation and **covenant**, and to express and embody God's atoning for their sins. On the other hand, he has what we would call a pastoral role, looking after people, sympathizing with them, getting alongside them and making the idea of the 'bridge' a reality in their experience. Of course, ordinary priests are themselves sinners, and must therefore offer sacrifices in relation to their own sins as well as those of the people.

This creates the double context which the writer will now explore. First, Jesus is the culmination of this idea of priesthood. He is the priest par excellence. Second, however, he is far superior to any previous priest. He can do all that they do – including sympathizing with human weakness – but he belongs to a different sort of priesthood, one which we can rely on totally and for ever. This continues to be the main theme for the next three chapters, and it bears a good deal of pondering. Do you really dare to lean all the weight of your **faith** and hope on Jesus? Do you trust him that much?

HEBREWS 5.4–10

The Son Becomes the Priest

[4]Nobody takes the office of priesthood on himself; you have to be called by God, just as Aaron was. [5]In the same way, the Messiah didn't exalt himself so that he might become a high priest. The one who put him forward was the one who said to him,

> You are my son; today I have become your father,

[6]as he says in another passage,

> You are a priest for ever, according to the order of Melchizedek.

[7]During the time of Jesus' earthly life, he offered up prayers and supplications, with loud shouts and tears, to the one who was able to save him from death. He was heard because of his devotion. [8]Although he was a son, he learned the nature of obedience through what he suffered. [9]When he had been made complete and perfect, he became the source of eternal salvation for all who obey him, [10]since he has been designated by God as a high priest according to the order of Melchizedek.

A man I know inherited a business from his father. It sounds rather a grand sort of thing: the son comes in, fresh from his excellent schooling, to sit in a splendid office next to that of his father, and to take over in due course, ruling the company from above, enjoying the lifestyle of business lunches, golf outings, foreign trips, and all the rest.

It actually wasn't a bit like that. For a start, it happened at a time of great austerity, when there wasn't any spare cash for even the occasional lavish lunch, let alone trips and outings. What was more, the father made sure the son learned the business from the ground up. He had to work in the workshops along with hardened mechanics. He had to visit the suppliers to see where the raw materials came from, and find out for himself how hard it was to get them at the right price. He had to go out as a salesman into the suspicious world that wasn't convinced it wanted the product in the first place. And he had to share the work of the financial department as they spent day after day crunching the complicated numbers that told the story of success or failure. Only when he had thoroughly understood every aspect of how the business worked was he even given an office of his own. And that was only the beginning. Now he would have to learn both how to lead and how to manage a workforce at a time of growing industrial unrest, as well as to represent the business in the wider world of local and national life and politics. He had to learn what it meant to be the son of his father. Nature put him in the frame for this, but a good deal of nurture was needed as well.

This goes some way towards explaining one of the oddest phrases in the whole letter, which comes here in verse 8. Although Jesus was God's son, he 'learned the nature of obedience through what he suffered'. One might have thought (the writer seems to be saying) that being God's son would simply be a matter of sharing God's rule of the world, living in glory and bliss. Not so. The God who is the father of Jesus is the God who made the world in the first place, and he remains deeply committed to his creation, even though it has become wayward and corrupt. If Jesus is to be his son, he must learn what this creation business is about, what it will take to rescue it from the mess it has got itself into. He must get to know its

48

depths as well as its heights. He must learn what it means to be his father's obedient son; and that will mean suffering, not because God is a sadist who simply wants to see his dear son having a rough time of it, but because the world which God made and loves is a dark and wicked place and the son must suffer its sorrow and pain in order to rescue it.

That's what verse 9 means when it says that Jesus was 'made complete and perfect' (it's just one word in the Greek). It doesn't mean that he was 'imperfect' before in the sense of being sinful, but that he needed to attain the full stature of sonship through experiencing the pain and grief of the father himself over his world gone wrong. He became truly and fully what in his nature he already was.

This demand for the son to learn what sonship truly means in practice is at the heart of his qualification for, so to speak, the other half of his mandate. The author of Hebrews, like many other early Christian thinkers, brought together biblical passages which spoke of the **Messiah** as God's son with one particular Psalm, Psalm 110, which spoke of him also as a **priest**. Here, in verse 5, he quotes (as he did in 1.5) from Psalm 2.7, where God says to the newly installed king of Israel, 'you are my son; today I have become your father'. But now he links it with Psalm 110.4, which adds a new and unexpected role: the Messiah is also to be a priest, and a priest of a different 'order', a different type or rank, the 'order of Melchizedek'.

This is the point at which many readers think to themselves, 'Well, that's me finished; I'll never understand this stuff.' It's comforting that in the verse which begins the next passage (verse 11) the writer anticipates precisely this reaction. He knows it's going to be difficult, but if we stick with him he will explain it step by step. (He also has some rather sharp remarks about the level of our understanding, and encourages us to grow up so we can understand the finer points he wants to make!) But for the moment we should be on solid ground. Psalm 110, one of the most frequently quoted Psalms in the New Testament, begins with the passage quoted in 1.13: 'YHWH said to my Lord, "Sit at my right hand, until I make your enemies a stool for your feet."' This fits in with the use of Psalm 8 which we've already seen in chapter 2, where the Messiah has everything 'put in subjection under his feet'. Hebrews is now exploring further within the same Psalm, looking at the fact that God has appointed Jesus to be a priest of this new type.

The present passage stresses that this appointment was God's own doing, not something that Jesus dreamed up for himself. The writer seems to be aware that people may have criticized the early Christian movement, and Jesus himself, for apparently snatching at a position which belonged, uniquely and for ever, to the **Temple** in Jerusalem and to the officials (**high priests**, priests and all the rest) who served there. It will indeed become clear that the Christian belief about Jesus upstages, and thus makes redundant, the Temple and all that goes on there, and the present argument is one step towards that conclusion. But the point of the present passage is that the priesthood which Jesus holds, because he is the Messiah, was always intended by God. The scriptures make it clear that, when God eventually sent the Messiah, he intended to make him a priest, and a new sort of priest at that.

The possible suggestion of arrogance, or of aloof superiority, is again undercut by the extraordinary picture of Jesus in verse 7. The writer clearly knows the stories of Jesus in the garden of Gethsemane, told in Mark 14.32–42 and the equivalent passages in Matthew and Luke; and he retells the story with the vivid detail of Jesus' 'loud shouts and tears' as he prayed in increasing agony that he might be spared the coming fate. This is the point at which, as verse 8 makes clear, he had to learn what the full extent of obedience would mean: he was praying 'to the one who was able to save him from death', but, though God could have saved him, he did not. The answer to his prayer for rescue was No. Or rather, the answer was that the prayer itself turned, as prayer often does, into acceptance: 'Your will be done.' Only so could Jesus discover the full meaning of sonship. Only so could he become the high priest that God had destined him to be, able to sympathize with us in our darkest moments.

HEBREWS 5.11–14

Are You Ready for Solid Food?

[11]I have plenty to say about all this; but it may be hard to make it clear, because your capacity to take things in has become sluggish. [12]Yes: by now you really should have become teachers, but you need someone to teach *you* the basic elementary beginnings of God's oracles. You need milk, not solid food! [13]Everyone who drinks milk, you see, is unskilled in the word of God's justice; such people are just babies. [14]Mature people need solid food – and by 'mature' I mean people whose faculties have been trained, by experience, to distinguish good from evil.

I saw in the newspaper this morning a delightful photograph of a Nepalese royal baby. The Kingdom of Nepal suffered a severe blow a few years ago when a member of the royal family shot dead several of his relatives. Now, with a new generation being born, the family is beginning to be restored. Hope is starting to emerge after the terrible shock and ordeal.

The photograph showed the baby, who as I write is six months old, being fed some solid food for the first time. This is apparently a central ritual in the religious practice of the family. It will be some while before the baby can move away from a diet of mostly milk and some small, soft solids to the fuller solid diet of the growing child. But a start has been made, and everyone was all smiles at the thought.

So why is it, in the twenty-first century as in the first, that so many Christians are not only eager to stay with a diet of milk, but actually get cross at the suggestion that they should be eating something more substantial? This is a question that has puzzled and bothered me for years. In my own country I meet a settled prejudice, even among people who are highly intelligent in other areas, who work in demanding professions, who read serious newspapers and magazines and who would be ashamed not to know what was going on in the world, against making any effort at all to learn what the Christian **faith** is about. As a result we find, both inside the churches and outside, an extraordinary ignorance of who Jesus really was, what Christians have believed and should believe about God and the world, how the entire Christian story makes sense, what the Bible contains, and, not least, how individual Christians fit in, and how their lives and their thoughts should be transformed by the power of the **gospel**. There are many places in the world where there is a great hunger to know all these things, and an eagerness to grasp and take in as much teaching as one can. Some Christians are indeed eager and ready for solid food. But I deeply regret that, in many churches in Western Europe at least, it seems that the most people can be persuaded to take on board is another small helping of warm milk.

So I have something of a fellow-feeling for what the writer to the Hebrews says in this sudden and surprising passage. He must have known his audience quite well, both to be able to make this analysis of where they were spiritually and intellectually and to have the courage to say it straight to them. He has some more comforting things to say later on; but this remarkable rebuke bursts upon us, and must have burst upon its first hearers, like a sudden cold shower. He clearly wants to wake them up with his double challenge.

First, he accuses them of being 'sluggish' in their capacity to take things in. If you've ever tried to explain something complicated to a class of pupils at the end of a long hard day, when they are all tired and longing to be off home, you'll know what he felt like. He knew it was important for them to take in what he was saying, but he could just imagine the glazed look on their faces and the lazy inclination to say, 'How about something a bit easier?' In our churches today we need to recognize this same tendency. It's one thing for people who are genuinely young in the faith, or are genuinely tired out and need a good rest, to say 'Let's keep it simple and easy'. It's quite another thing for people who have been Christians for some time, and show every other sign of being capable of learning and growing in the faith, to say, or imply, 'We're too lazy to do that.'

Let's not fool ourselves. Learning more about the Christian world-view, the large map on which we live, and more and more smaller bits of it, is a way of growing in strength in our praying, our living, our work for the gospel in whatever we do. Holding back from such learning, perhaps with the false humility of 'I'm not good at understanding these things' when we really mean 'I can't be bothered to try', is a way of saying that we want to remain spiritual babies. The writer tells them that they ought by now to be teachers, but they still need someone else to teach *them*! He clearly implies that within quite a short time a Christian community, and the individuals within it, ought to grow up to the stage that they can themselves instruct those who are younger in the faith. They ought to have been on solid food some time ago, but they still seem to need more milk.

What is the maturity, then, which he has in mind? This is the second half of his bracing challenge. People who are ready for 'solid food' are people who are 'skilled in the **word** of God's justice' (verse 13), people who have had their spiritual, intellectual and emotional faculties trained by experience and practice to tell good from evil (verse 14). The word for 'justice' is a tricky one wherever we meet it in the New Testament; it's often translated 'righteousness', but that gives people the impression that it's all about behaving yourself in a rather self-consciously religious fashion, which certainly isn't what Hebrews (or the other early Christians) had in mind. 'Justice' doesn't quite catch the full flavour, either, but at least it makes the point that the purposes of God in the gospel are focused on God's longing to put the world to rights, and to put people to rights as part of that work. What the writer here longs for is that people should become proficient in understanding and using the entire **message** of God's healing, restoring, saving justice. He wants them to know their way around the whole message of scripture and of the gospel, to be able to handle this message in relation to their own lives, their communities and the wider world, and to see how all the different parts of God's revelation fit together, apply to different situations and have the power to transform lives and situations.

In particular, he wants to see grown-up Christianity: people and communities who have learned, in the only way possible, how to tell right from wrong. Just as a child learns, or ought to learn, that some things are good and others bad (and learning this is part of the process of human maturity), so the Christian individual, and the Christian community as a whole in any church or place, should expect to grow up to maturity in discovering the difference between what is appropriate behaviour for a Christian and what is inappropriate. It isn't so much that the writer has as his principal aim a desire to get them to change their behaviour. That is nowhere suggested in the letter. Rather, he is highlighting this sign of maturity as a way of reminding them that there *is* such a thing as maturity, that they should be seeking it, and that mature people normally need, and indeed prefer, solid food rather than a purely liquid diet. The message for us should be clear. If we find ourselves wanting to turn away from the challenge to think harder about our faith, we should ask ourselves whether we are really prepared to settle for permanent spiritual babyhood.

HEBREWS 6.1–8

No Way Back

[1]So let's leave the basic level of teaching about the Messiah, and go on towards maturity! (Let's not repeat the performance of laying a foundation of repentance from dead works and faith towards God, [2]teaching about baptisms, laying on of hands, the resurrection of the dead and eternal judgment.) [3]We shall do this, if God allows us to.

[4]For once people have been enlightened – when they've tasted the heavenly gift and have had a share in the Holy Spirit, [5]and have tasted the good word of God and the powers of the coming age – [6]it's impossible to restore them again to repentance if they fall away, since they are crucifying God's son all over again, on their own account, and holding him up to contempt. [7]You see, when rain falls frequently on the earth, and the land drinks it up and produces a crop useful to the people for whom it's being cultivated, it shares in God's blessing. [8]But if it produces thorns and thistles, it's useless, and not far off from being cursed. What happens in the end is that it will be burned up.

I have a vivid memory of learning my ABC. Actually, I learned to read a bit before I went to school, but during my first weeks there I remember the whole class, all 50 of us, singing through the alphabet to a well-known tune. We liked our young teacher and did it well for her. Sometimes today, when I'm looking up a word in a dictionary and flicking to and fro between different letters of the alphabet, I hear that song in the back of my mind, and I am grateful for a good, cheerful start to my education.

But what would my university tutors have said, 15 years later, if I had requested that, instead of tutorials on philosophy and ancient history, I could be allowed to sing that alphabet song over and over again? They would have thought either that it was a student prank or simply that I had gone mad. You learn the alphabet early on, not so that you can forget it and learn it over and over again, but so that from that moment on you can take it for granted.

The writer of Hebrews is working his way round to saying, 'If you're prepared to grow up to maturity, here's some strong meat for you to get your teeth into!' As he prepares them for further teaching, he issues a stern warning about the impossibility of giving people a second start in the Christian **faith** if they turn round the first time and trample on it. His main point is that when you've learnt the ABC of the Christian faith you must go on from there. You can't go backwards, any more than you can set off on a bicycle and then, a minute later, cycle backwards to where you began and start off again. If you try to do that, you'll fall off, which is more or less what verse 6 says.

Before we discover why Hebrews says this, and what exactly the writer means, let's take a closer look at how he describes Christian beginnings and basic Christian teaching.

Verses 4 and 5 offer a lavish description of what happens when you become a Christian. First, you are 'enlightened'. You come to 'see the light' with your mind's eye, to recognize the truth about God, the world, yourself and your neighbour.

Second, you 'taste the heavenly gift'. You begin to experience a new kind of **life** and love which reaches out and embraces you, and you realize that this life and love come from **heaven**, from God himself.

Third, you have a share in the **holy spirit**. This is a more personal way of speaking about how the one God comes to the individual and community, revealing truth, assuring us of love, awakening hope.

Fourth, you 'taste the good **word** of God'. You experience the Bible, and the **message** about Jesus, like a long cool drink on a hot day, or like solid food when you hadn't realized how hungry you were.

Fifth, you also taste 'the powers of the coming age'. The new creation which God will one day accomplish has already begun in Jesus, and a sense of that newness steals over you, making you long both that the new world will come to birth very soon and that you will be made ready for it.

The writer assumes that, though his readers are still only babies, needing milk not solid food, they would be able to nod with recognition to all of these. If, today, we don't regard them as foundational for our Christian experience, what's gone wrong?

Similar questions arise when we look at his description of the Christian ABC, the rudimentary teachings which he shouldn't have to repeat. Here they are in verses 1 and 2.

First, **repentance** from dead works. This refers both to the religious practices of paganism (the worship of idols and all that it involves) and the behaviour characteristic of pagan society. In Hebrews, the phrase also hints at the continuation of the Jewish **Temple** rituals, which have become redundant with the achievement of Jesus.

Second, faith towards God. This is spelled out more fully in

11.1 and 11.6. It means, of course, belief and trust in the one true God as opposed to idols.

Third, teaching about **baptisms** and laying on of hands. This double action was, from the earliest times, associated with admission into the Christian community. Jesus' movement began with **John**'s baptism, and from the earliest days of the church new converts received baptism, followed by the laying on of hands, as the sign and means of their sharing in the new common life of the Christian family.

Fourth, the **resurrection** of the dead and eternal judgment (or perhaps we should translate it 'the judgment of the coming age'). Again, from earliest times the Christians were quite clear that there would come a time when God would judge the whole world and usher in the **age to come**. No vague hope for 'a better by and by'; no sense that, after death, one's behaviour in the present life won't seem to matter so much. Rather, a very specific hope, solidly rooted in long-standing Jewish tradition and given fresh focus and impetus by Jesus' own resurrection.

At this point, once more, many modern Christians will rub their eyes in surprise. These are the . . . basics? The original early Christian ABC? Most of our congregations don't know much about them! Many in our churches today couldn't tell you why we baptize people, what precisely the resurrection is and why they should believe in it, let alone what 'dead works' are and why you should repent of them. If this is the alphabet of Christian education, I fear there are many churches, as well as individual Christians, that need to go back to primary school. It's not, I think, that they've learned the alphabet long ago and forgotten it. No: they haven't ever learned it in the first place. They are getting by on the spiritual equivalent of grunts and hand signals.

The point of this list is for the writer to say that he is *not* going to go back over all this ground again. Rather, he wants to go deeper, to teach them more developed and wide-ranging truths. And the solemn warning about 'falling away' in verses 4–8 fits here as a way of saying that if you have learned the ABC thoroughly, and have started off enthusiastically on the Christian path, you can't expect to be restored if you then renounce it and go off in a different direction. As with the child who, having learnt the ABC, refuses either to read, write or even speak intelligibly, the teacher comes to suspect that nothing is ever going in, or at least that it's not doing any good.

That is the picture we have in verses 7 and 8. The land gets watered, and produces a crop. But if the only crop is thorns and thistles (this echoes Genesis 3.18, where thorns and thistles are a sign of the fall) then the farmer will give up hope, and eventually turn the whole thing into a bonfire. But what could a Christian individual or community do that would be the equivalent of such a thing?

When he speaks of 'falling away', and of 'crucifying God's son all over again', the writer seems to have in mind people who have belonged to the church, who have taken part in its common life, but who then decide it isn't for them, abandon their membership, and join in the general public contempt for the faith. This raises an interesting question, which the writer doesn't pursue here: is it possible first to become a genuine Christian and then to lose everything after all? To this question Paul, in Romans 5—8, gives the emphatic answer 'No!', and advances detailed arguments to prove the point. In the present passage the writer quickly goes on to say that he doesn't think his readers come into the category he's describing, but he doesn't unpack the wider theological question. The normal way of holding what he says together with what Paul and others imply is that the people described in verses 4 and 5 are people who have become church members, and have felt the power of the **gospel** and the life that results from it through sharing the common life of Christian fellowship, but who have never really made it their own, deep down inside. When he says in 12.15, 'Take care that nobody lacks God's grace,' he seems to envisage such a category of people. But he doesn't press the point. Nor should we press him for answers to questions he wasn't asking.

We should, rather, let him pose his sharp and uncomfortable question directly to us. Are we – or are some within our Christian fellowship – in danger of turning our backs on the faith, and joining in the general tendency to sneer at the gospel and the church? Are we lining up with those who hold firm to their original faith and hope, or with those who, like Peter by the charcoal fire, are ready to deny that they have anything to do with Jesus?

HEBREWS 6.9–12

Keep Up the Good Work

[9]Even though I speak in this way, my dear people, I am confident that there are better things to be said about you, things that point to salvation. [10]God is not unjust, after all – and he'd have to be if he forgot your work, and the love you showed for his name, and all the service you have rendered and are still rendering to his people. [11]I want to encourage each one of you to show the same energetic enthusiasm for the task of bringing your hope to its full, assured goal. [12]You mustn't become lazy. There are people who are inheriting the promises through faith and patience, and you should copy them!

Sir Francis Drake was one of many Englishmen who became famous during the reign of Elizabeth I. He sailed round the world, crossed the Atlantic many times, was involved in numerous sea battles in various parts of the world, was twice a member of parliament, and, perhaps most famously, defeated the Spanish armada when it came to attack England in 1588. There are many well-known stories about him: how he insisted on finishing his game of bowls even though the armada was in sight; how he spread his cloak over a muddy puddle so that the queen could walk over it without getting her feet wet; how he once tried to claim California as a British possession.

Not so well known, perhaps, but significant in revealing one of the secrets of his life, filled as it was with remarkable achievements, is a prayer he wrote which is still in frequent use in churches today. It sums up more or less exactly the message of this passage from the middle of Hebrews 6:

O Lord God, when thou givest to thy servants to endeavour any great matter, grant us also to know that it is not the beginning, but the continuing of the same, until it be thoroughly finished, which yieldeth the true glory; through him who for the finishing of thy work laid down his life for us, our Redeemer, Jesus Christ. Amen.

What Drake said there about great works which had to be attempted – he might have been thinking of another long and dangerous sea voyage, or the numerous tasks he undertook to improve the lot of people living in south-west England – Hebrews says about the entire enterprise of living as a Christian. What matters is not so much the beginning, important though that obviously is, but continuing, carrying on until the thing is thoroughly finished.

Most of us will recognize the picture and its challenge. Most of us have started projects and got bogged down: learning a new language, trying to lose weight, painting a picture, reading a long and difficult book. Or even, we might add, starting a business, opening a shop or building a house. Often we discover, some way into such projects, that we really aren't cut out for such things, and then it may be better to put it aside rather than carry on and make things worse. But often, not least when something is really worthwhile, there are several distinct phases to the process: the initial burst of enthusiasm and the excitement of something quite new, the gradual seeping away of energy as we reach the hard grind of carrying on, and then the days, and perhaps the weeks and even years, when we get out of bed without enthusiasm, without desire to work on the project, wishing we could have some other novelty to excite us, but realizing that there is a goal ahead which will make it all worthwhile if only we can put one foot in front of another until we get there.

Living as a Christian is often like that, and the writer of Hebrews knows that his readers may be in just that situation. They began well, and by this stage they had already established an impressive track record of service to God and to one another. The picture of Christian life in verse 10 is attractive: a community devoted to hard work in order to put into practice the love which is at the centre of genuine Christian **faith**, serving one another and all God's people in every way possible. This sort of thing is solid evidence that their beginning was real, that they certainly do belong to God's people; and, according to verses 9 and 10, that God has already taken note of what they've been doing and won't let them fall away at this point. But at the same time – and here is the mystery at the heart of Christian perseverance – just because God will not forget what they've already done, they themselves must make every effort, must avoid all temptations to be lazy, must continue with the life of faith and patience 'until it be thoroughly finished'. They should take note of other people who are doing so (verse 12), and do their best to copy them.

This strange balance between God's faithfulness and human effort needs a word or two of further explanation. Ever since the Reformation in the sixteenth century, many Christians have been taught, quite rightly, that nothing we can do can earn God's favour. Grace remains grace; God loves us because he loves us, not because we manage to do a few things to impress him, or to notch up a few points on some heavenly scorecard. But at the same time the whole New Testament, from the teaching of Jesus in the **gospels**, through the **message** of Paul in his letters, and on to letters like Hebrews and James and the great book of Revelation, insists that what Christians *do*, having already been grasped by God's free love and grace, and relying in prayer and faith on further grace for every step of the way, matters a great deal. Living as a Christian is never a matter of settling back and 'letting God do it all'.

Yes, there are undoubtedly times when, like the children of Israel standing beside the Red Sea, we need the message that says, 'The Lord will fight for you; all you need to do is to be still' (Exodus 14.14). But these are the exceptional moments, the particular situations, often in times of emergency, when there is nothing we can or should do, and we must trust that God will do it all. But the normal Christian life is one of energy, enthusiasm, faithful effort and patient hard work. It is tragic when people are deceived, by an insistence that God must do it all, into a lazy attitude which shrugs its shoulders and refuses to lift a finger.

Of course – and here Paul and Hebrews are equally insistent – when people patiently work hard both at serving one another and at their own holiness of life, they will usually be aware, and if they aren't they must remind themselves, of where the energy comes from. When Paul tells the Philippians to 'work out their own salvation with fear and trembling', he at once adds, 'because God is at work in you' (Philippians 2.12–13). The energy to do all that we are called to do comes itself from God working within us in the power of the **holy spirit**. The spirit applies to our lives the promises of God in the past (that's the subject of the next section) and the completed work of Jesus the **Messiah**. This work goes down into our thoughts, our imaginations and (not least) our wills. That's the mystery – the same mystery, of divine and human action, which we meet at so many points of Christian thinking and living.

The important thing, then, is not to wait until you *feel like* living a holy life, or loving your neighbour, or working at the project of Christian service to which you are called and on which you've made a start. Your feelings are as unreliable as tomorrow morning's weather (I write as an Englishman used to changeable weather all year round, not as, say, a southern Californian knowing that the next day, like the previous one, will be sunny and warm!). What matters is the call of the gospel, the promise of God, and your task of being faithful and patient in the present: 'Until it be thoroughly finished'.

HEBREWS 6.13–20

God's Unchangeable Promise

[13]When God was making his promise to Abraham, you see, he had nobody else greater than himself by whom he could swear, and so he swore by himself, [14]with the words, 'I will most surely bless you, and multiply you very greatly.' [15]And so in this way Abraham, after much patience, obtained the promise. [16]People regularly swear by someone greater than themselves, and in all their disputes the oath confirms the matter and brings it to

> closure. [17]So when God wanted to show all the more clearly to the heirs of the promise just how unchangeable his will was, he guaranteed it with an oath, [18]so that through two unchangeable things, in which it is impossible that God should tell a lie, those of us who have come for refuge should have solid encouragement to take hold of the hope which lies before us. [19]We have this hope like an anchor, secure, solid, and penetrating into the inner place behind the curtain, [20]where Jesus has gone in ahead of us and on our behalf, having become a high priest for ever according to the order of Melchizedek.

'What's that, then?'

The little boy tugged at my hand and pointed to a large, ugly metal object prominently displayed near the front of the ship which was gliding by.

I took him a little further along the quay, and we came to another ship which was tied up alongside. From the same place in the bows there was a thick metal cable reaching down into the murky water below.

'It's the anchor,' I said. 'They drop it down when they want to stop and stay still. It sinks down deep into the mud at the bottom. Then even when it's windy and the tide gets high the ship won't move. When they want to sail again they haul it up, and there it is on the side.'

He looked at the ship as it moved away from us, out towards the open sea.

'Do all ships have one?' he asked.

'I think so,' I replied. 'You'd be in bad shape without it.'

Actually, in the only other place in the New Testament where anchors are mentioned, they were in bad shape even though they had several. The passage is Acts 27, which tells the story of Paul's voyage which ended in shipwreck on Malta. So when Hebrews tells us that the Christian hope acts like an anchor it is, as far as we know, the only time in early Christian writing when this idea is used. And it's made all the odder when the writer says that this anchor 'penetrates into the inner place behind the curtain'. Anchors belong on the sea bed, not behind a curtain! What on earth is he talking about?

Well, it isn't actually on earth; it's in **heaven**, and that's the point. He is working back to explaining, in the next chapter, what it means to speak of Jesus as a **high priest** 'according to the order of Melchizedek'. Because he's thinking of the high priest, he thinks of the **Temple**; and because he's thinking of what the high priest does in the Temple, his mind goes naturally (for a Jewish thinker) to the great moment, once a year, when the high priest goes in, behind the last curtain, into the innermost sanctuary of the Temple, the 'holy of holies'. There, on what they believed was the holiest spot on earth, the place where you were as close as possible to God himself, the high priest would make atonement for the people.

What he's going to say, more fully, in the passages to come is that Jesus has gone in, not into the earthly Temple in Jerusalem, but into the true sanctuary, the world of heaven itself, right into the innermost courts and into the very presence of the loving father. And he has gone there on our behalf. We are attached to him as though by a great metal cable. He is there, in the very presence of God, like an anchor. As long as we don't let go of the cable, we are anchored to the presence of God; all the winds, tides and storms that may come can't shift us. There is enormous comfort to be had, precisely at such times, in the knowledge that the anchor is 'secure and solid' (verse 19). (As I write this, I am very aware of two friends both of whom have lost adult sons this week to sudden and unexplained death; sometimes the storms are overwhelming.) We are not promised that there won't be any storms; indeed, the provision of a secure anchor implies that there will be. What we are promised is that we will be kept safe.

This is the promise which lies underneath the appeal of the last two sections, the appeal to stand firm and hold on patiently. The rest of our present passage, leading to this climactic statement, explores the way in which Abraham, the classic biblical example of faithful patience, hung on to God's promises through thick and thin. And it explains, in particular, why Abraham knew – and why we should know – that God means what he says, that the promises are as solid and unbreakable as they could possibly be. When God made the promises, he swore that he would keep them, not by anyone else, but by his own self.

This, like the anchor, isn't obvious at first sight. It's difficult to translate the words of the promise in verse 14, and we can't at once see how it is in fact an oath which God swears by his own character. In fact, the words 'I will most surely bless you' are, more literally, 'If I don't surely bless you . . .'. This is the clue: the sentence is part of an implied longer one. It is as though you or I were to say, 'If I don't keep this promise, may I never be trusted again,' and then to miss out the last words, simply saying, 'If I don't keep this promise . . .'. God is saying, 'If I don't surely bless you, may my name be mud for ever.' Strong stuff, you may think; and that is exactly the point Hebrews is making. First, God made promises to Abraham; then he swore an oath that he would indeed keep them. 'Two unchangeable things', as verse 18 puts it. God can't lie in either of them.

This is why the promise can and must be regarded as firm and secure; and this, in turn, explains what lies underneath the exhortations in the previous passage, to hold on to hope and to persevere in **faith**. Doing this isn't whistling in the dark. We don't have faith in faith, as people sometimes suggest. Christian hope isn't optimism, a vague sense that things will probably turn out all right. Christian faith is trusting – and going on trusting through thick and thin – in the God who made unbreakable promises and will certainly keep them. Christian hope is looking ahead to the time when, according to those promises, God will make the world over anew, completing the work he began in Jesus. And it's Jesus on whom the whole thing rests. That's why Christians tell the story of Jesus over and over again, day by day and (in the liturgical sequence of the year which many churches follow) year by year.

Holding on to that story is like making sure the anchor's cable is firmly attached at our end. But the point of it all is that the anchor itself is secure and solid. The reason the writer of this letter is now going to explore the deeper and stranger truth about Jesus as the true high priest is because this will give his readers, ourselves included, all the more encouragement to trust and hope. We shall be needing it.

HEBREWS 7.1–10

Melchizedek, the Great Priest-King

[1]For this Melchizedek, 'king of Salem, priest of the most high God, met Abraham as he was coming back after defeating the kings, and blessed him; [2]and Abraham portioned out to him a tenth of everything.'

To begin with, if you translate Melchizedek's name, it means 'king of righteousness'; then he is also 'king of Salem', which means 'king of peace'. [3]No mention is made of his father or mother or genealogy, nor of the beginning or end of his earthly life. He is described in a similar way to the son of God; and he continues as a priest for ever.

[4]Look and see what an exalted status he has. Abraham the patriarch gave him a tenth of the spoils! [5]Those of Levi's sons who receive the priesthood have a command to take tithes from the people according to the law – from, that is, their own brothers and sisters, although they, too, are physical descendants

of Abraham. ⁶But this man, who doesn't share their genealogy at all, received tithes from Abraham, and blessed the man who possessed the promises. ⁷It is beyond all question that the lesser is blessed by the greater. ⁸In the former case, mortal humans receive tithes; in the latter case, the one who received them was one of whom scripture declares that he is alive. ⁹And, if I can put it like this, even Levi paid tithes through Abraham – Levi, the one who receives tithes! ¹⁰He was still in his ancestor's loins, you see, when Melchizedek met him.

I was telephoned by a Christian magazine a few months ago. They were running a feature on various writers and they wanted to know, among many other questions, which books I regarded as the most important in my thinking and my work.

As often when I'm asked unexpected questions, my mind went blank for a minute. Then I looked around my study. I realized at once that the most important books to me, day by day and week by week, were not the great novels, plays and poems, much as I love them. Nor – to the surprise, I think, of the feature writer – were they the works of the great theologians and biblical scholars, much though I am indebted to many of them. No: the books that I treasure most, that I would be sorriest to be parted from, the ones that are always within reach, are the big reference books: a classical dictionary, a dictionary of the Christian church, a dictionary of biography, various atlases, encyclopedias of philosophy, archaeology, art, history and so on. And, of course, various dictionaries of biblical themes, people and topics; and, along with all of that, dictionaries of the ancient languages, particularly Hebrew and Greek. I love the thought that within arm's reach is a whole world of learning, or at least the gateway to it, pointing me to other books both ancient and modern.

What normally happens is this. I am working on a particular subject and I come across something – a topic, a place, a name – I don't know anything about (this happens, naturally, many times a week). I am puzzled about it: if the reference is in a text, it means I can't grasp what the text as a whole is saying. Then I go to the relevant dictionary, and perhaps to the other books that the dictionary tells me to look up. Suddenly, from a small question about a single person or topic, a whole new area of thought, history or culture opens up in front of me, and I can quite easily get lost in it for an hour or two. It is as though, through that small window of a single word or person, I can get a view of a wide sweep of the ancient world. Then, remembering what I'm supposed to be doing, I come back to my work; only now I can carry with me, as I read the original text I was working on, all the information about that one person or topic. Again and again I am rewarded for my efforts as the text springs to life. What started off as a small puzzle in the middle of my work has turned into a lighthouse sending rays of light flashing over the rest of the subject.

That is the effect that Hebrews wants to create with this discussion of Melchizedek. This passage takes us into what seems at first sight a technical, almost bizarre discussion of the short reference to Melchizedek in the book of Genesis. It does so because, according to Psalm 110.4, the **Messiah**, the one to whom all things are put into subjection, is appointed by God as 'a **priest** for ever, after the order of Melchizedek'. The writer has quoted that passage, tantalizingly, three times already (5.6, 10; 6.20). Now at last Hebrews is doing for us what I do when, puzzled by something in a text, I reach for the relevant reference book and start to delve into a new area.

He, like many early Christians, has realized that Jesus has been appointed by God to a position at his right hand, waiting for his **kingdom** to be complete (Psalm 110.1). But he has asked himself the question which nobody else so far as we know had asked: what exactly did the same Psalm mean when it spoke of

Jesus' priesthood 'according to the order of Melchizedek'? So, as I reach for my dictionaries and encyclopedias, the writer reaches for the only other passage in the whole Bible where Melchizedek is mentioned, namely the fourteenth chapter of Genesis. What sort of priesthood did he have there? How did it relate to what God was promising to Abraham? What clues might there be to help us understand more about Jesus himself?

After quoting the key passage from Genesis 14.17–20, the writer goes on, almost musingly, to think for a start about what Melchizedek's name means. *Melech* in Hebrew means 'king'; *zedek* in Hebrew means 'righteousness' or 'justice'. Well then, he is 'king of righteousness'; and since he's 'king of Salem' (that is, Jerusalem), and since *shalom* means 'peace', he is also 'king of peace'. But this is really just toying with possibilities. The real point is yet to come.

Verse 3, which is often misunderstood, is the heart of it, and to get the point we need to understand what was so striking, to any Jew, about the claim that the king spoken of in Psalm 110 would be, in any sense, a priest. Granted, Solomon had offered **sacrifices** in the **Temple**; but thereafter the kings, who were descended from the tribe of Judah, had not done so. There was a clear division: priests were from the tribe of Levi (and within that, more specifically, from the family of Aaron); kings were from the tribe of Judah. How then could a king be a priest as well? And, even if he was, what sort of relationship might there be between the two types of priesthood that would thus exist alongside one another?

Verse 3, translated literally, begins: 'Fatherless, motherless, genealogy-less, having neither beginning of days nor end of life'. Some people have thought that the writer, finding in the text no mention of Melchizedek's parents or his more distant ancestors, or his birth or death, is 'deducing' that he didn't have any of the above. This is unnecessary and unlikely. The point is much more obvious: Melchizedek is introduced into the story of Abraham, as a 'priest of God most high', but without any mention being made of *where he got his priesthood from*, more particularly of whether he obtained it by inheritance from his family. Nor is there any mention of his priesthood starting or finishing with birth or death. It is as though, in the story, he is just there, as something of a permanent fixture. This prepares us for the point which is rammed home in the next passage, about the fact that Jesus' high priesthood does not depend on being born into a priestly family, and that his priesthood, unlike that of the Levitical priests, continues uninterrupted to the present time.

Verses 4–10 then set out the contrast between the Levitical priesthood (which in the writer's day was still at work in the Temple in Jerusalem) and the priesthood which Psalm 110, explained in the light of Genesis 14, ascribes to Jesus. The priesthood 'after the order of Melchizedek', he says, is obviously superior, because even Abraham paid tithes to Melchizedek, and Melchizedek blessed him. He is thus superior not only to Abraham, but also to Levi, one of Abraham's great-grandchildren; Levi was in a manner of speaking already present, in the sense of being contained in his ancestor's body, when Melchizedek and Abraham met. We are thus prepared for the conclusion: Jesus himself, the Melchizedek-type **high priest**, is far superior to the present Levitical priesthood. This has a double result. On the one hand, Jesus has made the present Temple and all that goes with it redundant. On the other hand, we can put complete confidence and trust in him, as the true and lasting high priest. Discovering more about Melchizedek, and so discovering what the Psalm meant when talking of the Messiah as a priest as well as a king, is a way to increase and deepen our sense of trust and assurance as we lean the full weight of our future hope on Jesus and on him alone.

HEBREWS 7.11–19
A New Order of Priesthood

[11]So, you see, if it had been possible to arrive at complete perfection through the Levitical priesthood (for the people received the law by that means), what further need would there have been to speak of another priesthood being established 'according to the order of Melchizedek', rather than 'according to the order of Aaron'? [12]Change the priesthood, after all, and you're bound to change the law – [13]especially when you consider that the one of whom these things are spoken comes from another tribe altogether, one from which nobody is recruited to serve at the altar. [14]It's obvious, isn't it, that our Lord was descended from Judah, and Moses never made any connection between that tribe and the priesthood.

[15]This is even clearer when another priest arises 'according to the order of Melchizedek', [16]who attains this rank not because of a law concerning physical descent but through the power of a life that cannot be destroyed. [17]What scripture says about him, after all, is, 'You are a priest for ever, according to the order of Melchizedek.' [18]What is happening here is that the previous commandment is being set aside. It was, after all, weak and useless; [19]the law brought nothing to perfection, did it? Instead, what appears is a better hope, through which we draw near to God.

'I want it all to be *perfect*! There must be nothing wrong! Everything's got to be just right!'

The bride-to-be was getting more and more excited as the great day approached. Though many people in Western society scoff at the institution of marriage, many others, including a

73

great many young people, still see a wedding service as one of the high points, perhaps *the* high point, of their life. For much of the time, most of us live in comparative obscurity. Now, suddenly, two people take centre stage, with the people they know best and love most all around them. No wonder they want everything to be perfect. They don't want to look back and say 'Pity about the cake' or 'What a shame the dress wasn't quite right' or 'Too bad there was a leak in the church roof and the bridegroom got wet'.

But perfection doesn't just happen. You have to work at it, little bit by little bit. Take each aspect of the occasion: the clothes, say. You have to plan, months in advance; you have to speak to all the relevant people; there is measuring up to be done, fitting, standing back and looking, final decisions. The same goes for the food. And (though not everyone realizes this) the same goes for the wedding service itself: choosing exactly the right readings and music, the hymns and the prayers. Perfection is what you get when every aspect of every department of the whole event has been worked through, thought through, smoothed out and practised.

Hebrews has a lot to say about 'perfection', not least in this passage (see verses 11 and 19), but at first sight most of us find it difficult to figure out what exactly it means. The danger is that we'll imagine it's simply talking about *moral* perfection, which one might suppose was to be achieved by harder and harder moral effort until not only every wrong action but also every wrong thought and motive had been ironed out of our character. As most of us are all too aware, that is a long way off.

It appears on closer inspection, though, to be something subtly different. The 'perfection' in question could also be translated *completeness*; it's what you get when everything has been put into place for the final great purpose to be achieved. What is this great purpose? Nothing less, it seems, than God's intention for the whole created world. This includes human behaviour, but goes much wider. The world is God's great project. Just as a bride and bridegroom plan their wedding day, and work to make it perfect, God is working at bringing his world to perfection and doing what is necessary to make it complete.

For those who lived under the **law** of Moses, it would have been easy to suppose that the way to share in that great plan was simply to be part of the community that focused its life on the **Temple**, and relied on the **sacrifices** offered by the Levitical **priests**, descended from Aaron. Somehow, the ancient Israelites believed, God the creator would work through that means to bring Israel itself to perfection and thereby to bring perfection to the wider world. But it didn't happen that way – not least because God didn't intend it to. He had already promised, early on in the process, that there would come a time when the Levitical priesthood would be replaced with a different one altogether. The Levitical priests and their work pointed forward to the eventual 'perfection', but they couldn't, by themselves, bring it into reality.

They were part of a whole system which, as Hebrews has already argued at length, was designed by God not to be permanent but to point forward to what was to come. They were (in other words) part of the law of Moses, which the Levitical priests used to teach the people as part of their overall duties. But when Psalm 110 points forward to the coming king and assigns him a different type of priesthood, it clearly implies that there will be a change in the regime within which that priesthood functions and makes sense (verse 12). Verses 13 and 14 highlight one of the key points of difference, for which the earlier section of the chapter had prepared the way: Jesus was descended from the tribe of Judah, and in the Mosaic law there is no mention of people from that tribe being chosen as priests. Clearly there is an entire change of dispensation under way, which is where the argument will go in the next chapter.

The thrust of all this – it may seem somewhat technical, but, as any mechanic will tell you, unless someone pays attention to the technicalities you won't be able to drive the car down the road – is to celebrate the fact that, with the coming and achievement of Jesus, God has brought into being the 'perfection' which up until then had been impossible. Jesus, having died, has been raised from the dead and is alive for ever; he has brought into being 'the power of a **life** that cannot be destroyed' (verse 16). That means that those who belong to Jesus are not dependent for their spiritual health and hope upon a system that can't ultimately give perfection. We trust in the eternal, fully effective priesthood of the **son of God**, the **Messiah**. This is the 'better hope', through which we draw near to God (verse 19).

The word 'better' (or at least the Greek word which it here translates) occurs more times in Hebrews than in the whole of the rest of the New Testament put together. That tells us something about the way the writer thinks. He is constantly contrasting, not something bad with something good, but something good with something better. He is not saying that the ancient Israelite system was a bad thing, with its Temple, its law and its Levitical priesthood. What he is saying is that the new dispensation which has arrived in and through Jesus is *even better* than what went before. Now at last 'perfection' is in sight, and Jesus has achieved it for us. Let us then press on in **faith** and hope so that we may fully grasp the perfection, the glorious new world, which God has by this means prepared for us.

HEBREWS 7.20–28

The Permanent Priesthood of Jesus

[20]This is all the more so when you consider that an oath was sworn. The Levitical priests, you see, become priests without an oath, [21]but the Messiah attains his priesthood with an oath, through what was said to him:

> The Lord has sworn and will not repent;
> You are a priest for ever.

[22]Jesus has thus, additionally, become the guarantee of a better covenant.

[23]There needed to be a large number of Levitical priests, since they stop holding office at death. [24]But since he continues as a priest for ever, his priesthood is permanent. [25]That's why he is able to save those who come to God through him, completely and for ever – since he always lives to make intercession for them.

[26]It was appropriate that we should have a high priest like this. He is holy, without blame or stain, separated from sinners, and elevated high above the heavens. [27]He doesn't need (like the ordinary high priests do) to offer sacrifices every day, first for his own sins and then for those of the people. He did this once for all, you see, when he offered himself. [28]For the law appoints ordinary, weak, mortal men as high priests; but the word of the oath, which comes after the law, appoints the son, who has been made perfect for ever.

Many of the ancient parish churches in England have a board somewhere close to the door which lists all the rectors who have had charge of that parish. Often the list begins way back in the eighth or ninth century. Even when it's only the fifteenth or sixteenth century, so that the church stretches back five or six hundred years rather than over a thousand, it's still a remarkable feeling to read the names and to think of all those people, some no doubt holier than others, some no doubt wiser than others, who have, as best they could, served the people of that parish, preached God's **word** and administered the sacraments.

But where are they now? The answer is obvious; apart from the last one or two, or three or four at most, they are all dead and gone. They have held office for a time and are now, we trust, at rest – perhaps some of them in the very churchyard outside the building where we are standing. For the church to continue from generation to generation God has to raise up, again and again, people who will take on the calling to serve. They will pass away in their turn and others will succeed them. And so on.

But supposing, as we stood looking at the list, we discovered that someone had been appointed rector in, say, 1600, *and he was still there.* Somehow he had escaped the common lot of all the others, and the parish had never needed to replace him, because he was still alive, still a faithful minister of the **gospel.** An extraordinary and bizarre suggestion, of course – though we would all love to meet such a person, to talk to him about what life had been like for the last 400 years, the things the history books hadn't told us! But the real significance would come when you considered the question: what would it be like to have someone running the parish for 400 years?

Most church people would shrink from the idea, for the good reason that we know that nobody is perfect. By changing rectors regularly you hope to ensure that different skills are brought to the task, and different failings balanced out. But in this case the people would affirm that they were completely happy with the arrangement. The man was exactly what they needed. No further change was necessary.

The point of the present passage is that the long list of Levitical **priests** who ministered, both in the original wilderness tabernacle and then in the **Temple** in Jerusalem, was like that list of clergy who served a particular church. They all held office for a while and eventually they died. There had to be plenty of them, from generation to generation. But Jesus, by sharp contrast, 'continues as a priest for ever'. Once you reach him, the list comes to a stop. No more are needed. Nor is this a mere historical or theological curiosity. As with everything else our writer says about Jesus' priesthood, this point is there to reinforce the assurance that we can have through him. Jesus, the one who died for us and rose again, 'always lives to make intercession' for his people, for those 'who come to God through him'. No need to go any other route; in fact, no other route carries any promises of success. Jesus himself is the unique, human road into the very presence of God. When we get there we can rest, since our access to God in the first place, and our welcome when we arrive, is guaranteed for ever.

Once again, therefore, the very striking fact of God swearing an oath to confirm something is brought forward as part of the letter's assurance to its readers. God swore an oath to Abraham that he would indeed bless him with a great family, the family which now contains all those who come to God through Jesus. Verses 20–21 draw attention to the fact that Psalm 110 reports God swearing an oath that the **Messiah**, the coming king, will indeed be a priest according to the order of Melchizedek, not for a while only but for ever. And this, as the next three chapters will go on to explain, is the basis of the claim that in Jesus the **covenant** itself, the marriage bond between God and his people, has been renewed (verse 22).

Earlier on in the letter, in chapters 4 and 5, we noted one half of the meaning of Jesus' high priesthood. He is a truly human being, tempted in every respect just like we are, and he can therefore sympathize fully with our weakness and the pressures we find ourselves under. (Indeed, you could say that he knows more about it than we ever will, since we are inclined to yield to temptation and so never to face its full fury, whereas he, who never sinned, had to go on battling against it without the relief of giving in.) Now, in verses 26–28, we discover the other half of the picture. The priesthood of Jesus is like that of the other priests in the ways we need it to be, but it is *un*like theirs, too, in the ways we need it to be. He 'has been made perfect for ever' (verse 28), perfect in his fully qualified and effective priesthood, through which he has offered himself once and for all. This startlingly different **sacrifice** – nowhere in the Old Testament does a priest offer his own self! – will be explored in later chapters. The present point is the contrast between Jesus himself and the other priests. They went on sacrificing day after day and year after year; but part of the perfection, the completeness, of his priesthood is that he achieved in a single great sacrifice that to which all the previous sacrifices pointed but which they could never bring to perfection.

Some Christians face the danger of forgetting just how central and vital Jesus himself was and is to every aspect of Christian **faith**. It is possible to get so wrapped up in theological technicalities or practical details that Jesus comes into the equation, if at all, almost as an afterthought. Hebrews ought to provide a strong antidote to any such tendencies. This writer can't get enough of thinking through who Jesus was and is and what he achieved in his death and in the new **life** that emerged the other side. That alone is worth a good deal of pondering. When we then look at the details of the picture and realize the way in which he has brought to perfection, and so to a stop, the long line of earlier priests, pondering turns to gratitude, and gratitude to assurance and hope.

HEBREWS 8.1–6

Better Ministry, Better Covenant

¹The point of all this now appears. We have just such a high priest, who sat down at the right hand of the throne of the heavenly Majesty, ²as a minister of the holy things and of the true tabernacle, the one made by God rather than by humans.

³Every high priest, you see, is appointed in order to offer gifts and sacrifices, which is why this one, too, must have something to offer. ⁴If he were on earth, he wouldn't even be a priest, since there already are priests who make offerings in accordance with the law. ⁵They serve a copy and shadow of the heavenly realities, in line with what Moses was told, when he was getting ready to construct the tabernacle: 'take care that you make everything according to the pattern that was shown you on the mountain'. ⁶Now, you see, Jesus has obtained a vastly superior ministry. In the same way, he is the mediator of a better covenant, which is established on better promises.

When my sons were little, we gave them a game they could play at home. It was a type of football; except that you played it on a table top, with plastic figures an inch or two high. You had to flick them with your finger, so that they would hit the ball and try to get it into the opponent's goal in the usual way. It's not a bad game as far as it goes. You can become quite good at it, particularly if you're small and have active little fingers that learn how to flick the players in exactly the right way. But if you'd ever seen an actual football match you would never mistake the table-top variety for the real thing.

Supposing, however, that the game was given to a family that had not only never seen a real football match but who didn't know that such a thing existed. They might imagine that table-top football was the reality; this was all there was. They wouldn't know that it was a copy of the real thing, and

81

gained most of its meaning, and its appeal for most people, because it was reminding them of the true, grown-up version.

Something like this, only more so, lies at the heart of the contrast Hebrews now draws, and will go on drawing, between the **Temple** in Jerusalem, and/or the tabernacle which the Israelites had during their wilderness journeyings, and the true, or real, shrine, which is in . . . **heaven**. But this, like some other things in the letter, is difficult for us to grasp, and we need to pause and approach it slowly.

The trouble is that as soon as we hear someone talking about something in the present world being related to something 'in heaven', we are inclined to imagine the sort of contrast beloved by the Greek philosopher Plato, who thought that everything in the world of space, time and material objects was a copy, and a rather second-rate one at that, of things in the 'ideal' world, things which he called 'forms'. Lots of readers have imagined that Hebrews wants us to think in that way, too, about the earthly and the heavenly realities. But the meaning of 'heaven' and 'earth' in the Bible, not least in this book, is quite different from what Plato had in mind. For a start, we have already learned that Jesus has gone, still as a fully human being, *into* the world of heaven – something Plato could never have allowed. 'Heaven' is not, in the Bible, simply a 'spiritual', in the sense of 'non-physical', dimension; it is God's space, God's realm, which interlocks with our realm, our world ('earth') in all sorts of ways. And, just to make things one step more complicated again, the Israelites believed that the Temple in Jerusalem was the place above all where heaven and earth met, quite literally. When you went into the Temple, especially when you went into the holy of holies in the middle of it, you were actually going into heaven itself.

So when Hebrews talks about the Temple, or the wilderness

tabernacle, as a 'copy or shadow of the heavenly realities', the writer is careful to explain what he means. The original tabernacle, which accompanied the Israelites in the wilderness and continued as the centre of Israelite worship until the Temple was built by Solomon, was constructed, according to Exodus 25—31, on the basis of detailed instructions given by God himself to Moses. Indeed, according to the passage quoted here in verse 5 (Exodus 25.9, 40; we find similar things said in 26.30, 27.8, and Numbers 8.4), God actually *showed* Moses the heavenly sanctuary when he was on Mount Sinai. He let him look through the flimsy curtain that separates God's space and our space, so that Moses could see the true reality and be sure to have the earthly copy made in the right way. Then, later in the letter, we discover that this heavenly reality is part of the heavenly Jerusalem, to which all Jesus' followers already belong (12.22–24). All this (like much in this letter) is mysterious, indeed mind-boggling, but if we are to follow the thinking of the early Christians we must be patient.

This passage, in fact, draws together for the last time the contrast between Jesus as the true **high priest** and all the **priests** that have gone before him. It places this contrast inside two larger contrasts: the contrast of the earthly and temporary tabernacle or Temple and the true, heavenly one; and the contrast between the old **covenant**, the bond established on Mount Sinai between God and Israel, and the new covenant, promised long ago and now brought into being by Jesus. Verse 6, mentioning this latter point, introduces the new section of the letter which begins with verse 7.

The thrust of this conclusion, then, is that the readers must learn to distinguish between the copy and the reality – like small children discovering that there was such a thing as real live football, for which their table-top game was just a small substitute – and that they must learn to celebrate and enjoy the real thing, and not cling on to the copy. This must have presented a particular challenge to those Jewish Christians who all their lives had looked to the Jerusalem Temple as the focus of devotion, the place of pilgrimage, the very house of God, and to the priests who served in the Temple as God's representatives for all time. The challenge must have appeared as much political as theological; for much of the first century the Jews who lived in and around Jerusalem perceived themselves as being under threat, not least from Rome. Eventually the threat would burst out into an open war which would end with the destruction of Jerusalem and the Temple itself in AD 70. In such circumstances, anyone suggesting that the Temple was only a copy of the reality, and that anyone who came to God through Jesus was entering the true Temple which had all along existed in heaven and would one day be revealed as the reality, would be seen as horribly disloyal. And when countries and cultures are under threat, disloyalty is sometimes punished with violence . . .

As we shall see in chapter 10, that was indeed what had been happening. Part of the reason for writing the letter may well have been that the Jewish Christians who received it were under exactly that kind of pressure and threat, and needed to know, and to know very clearly, that the Jesus who they were following was indeed the true high priest, and had indeed entered the true Temple on their behalf. The old Temple was good; the new, real one was better. The old priests were good; the new Priest was better. The old covenant was good; the new one was better, established (verse 6) on better promises. As we look back to those early days, and put ourselves in the shoes, and the hearts, of our forebears in the Christian **faith**, we do well to ask ourselves whether our own devotion to Jesus, our own celebration of all that he is and has done, is as powerful and as central to our lives as the writer wanted him to be for his readers. If he was 'better' even than the Temple and its priesthood, how much more is he 'better' than the many things which so easily distract us from single-minded devotion to him.

HEBREWS 8.7–13

The Promise of a New Covenant

[7]If the first covenant had been faultless, you see, there wouldn't have been any reason to look for a second one. [8]God finds fault with them when he says:

See, says the Lord, the days are coming,
When I will complete, with the house of Israel,
With Judah's house, also, a covenant that's new:
[9]Not like the one which I made with their ancestors
On the day when I reached out and took them by the hand
To lead them away from the land of Egypt.
They didn't remain, after all, in my covenant,
And (says the Lord) I ceased to care for them.
[10]This is the covenant I will establish,
After those days with the house of Israel:
My laws will I place in their minds, says the Lord,
And write on their hearts; thus I shall be God
For all of them; they'll be my people indeed.
[11]No more will they need to instruct one another,
Or teach their own neighbours to know me, the Lord;
For from least unto greatest, each one shall know me,
[12]For I shall be merciful to their injustices
And as for their sins, I'll forget them for ever.

[13]Thus, when it speaks of a new covenant, it puts the first one out of date. And something that is out of date, and growing old, is about to disappear.

One of my favourite rivers is the Coquet, which rises in the heart of my native part of England, and runs down into the

North Sea about fifty miles south of the border with Scotland. It isn't a long river, even by national standards, let alone compared with the great rivers of Europe, still less the mighty Amazon or the Mississippi and Missouri. But at every point it has character and style. It begins as a bubbly mountain stream, collecting water from several sources high in the Pennines. It comes down into a winding valley, with pretty little villages and heather-covered hills. As it gets wider, so its valley gets deeper, passing an ancient monastery which is still used as a place of prayer and pilgrimage, and going down into gorges lined with leafy trees. As it reaches the sea, it comes under the shadow of an ancient castle, and, as though to celebrate its arrival at its destination, opposite its mouth is a small island which serves as a bird sanctuary. Many brooks and streams from several different hills contribute to it. Its character develops and changes as it goes to and fro. Many parts of it offer excellent fishing, and plenty of other wild creatures find homes nearby. It remains a single river, moving purposefully to its goal, even though you would hardly guess, from the tinkling stream, how deep a cutting it would eventually make, just as someone who only knew its final stretch, broadening to meet the incoming tide, would not easily imagine the steep rocks and hills where it all began.

We are nearly half way through Hebrews. As the thought of the letter is now going to cut deep into some rich theology, this is a good moment to look back over the route we have taken. Think back to the first excited and even bubbly celebration of the greatness of the **Messiah** over against the angels. Reflect on the many turns and twists of the biblical passages that have been called on and expounded, to the point we have now arrived at. Look on, as well, to the conclusion, the point where the now powerful river runs out into the sea, making its unique contribution to the larger reservoir of

Christian wisdom. As will be obvious from a glance at our present passage, we are now faced with the longest single biblical quotation we've had so far, in a book which has more than its fair share of them. This is an important clue as to how we should understand the flow of the book as a whole, in particular how the different streams of thought that contribute to the river play their part in making it what it is.

Remember how we noticed not long ago that the word 'better' occurs more in Hebrews than in the rest of the New Testament put together? That, too, provides a clue. What the writer is doing is choosing passages from the Old Testament which say, in effect: what we have is good, but God is doing something better. What we have is true, but it isn't the whole truth. What we know at the moment is important, but the most important thing we know is that God is planning to do something more. And the whole letter is written in order to say: the 'something more', the 'whole truth', the 'better thing', has now arrived in Jesus; so whatever you do, don't go back to the old things. However good and true they were, they are now taken up in the new and better. Otherwise you will look like someone trying to pump water from the river back into the various smaller streams from which it came. It can't be done. You must go where the river is taking you, even though it's travelling into countryside you hadn't expected.

Look back over the significant streams that have made the river what it is. We began, in the first two chapters, with a flurry of biblical passages all designed to say that Jesus, the Messiah, was God's one and only son, and as such greatly superior to the angels who gave the **law**. This blended with the discussion of Psalm 8 in chapter 2, where it became clear that Jesus is the truly human being who has already attained the sovereignty over creation which God intended for the whole human race. Then, in chapters 3 and 4, the writer took us into a different world, that of Psalm 95, insisting that according to the Psalm itself there is still a '**sabbath** rest' waiting for God's people, something for which the entry into the promised land was just an advance picture. This was meant to stimulate the readers into realizing that they must make every effort to hold on firmly to their **faith** and hope.

The mood then shifted at the end of chapter 4, as Hebrews focused on Jesus as the true **high priest**; we were thus introduced to Psalm 110, with its mention of Jesus as a **priest** 'according to the order of Melchizedek'. This has been the fullest example so far of the way the writer has used the Bible: finding a passage which points beyond itself, beyond its own times, to a reality yet to come. From early in chapter 5 to the middle of chapter 8, in the last passage we looked at, this has been the central theme, including a sharp word of warning about how important it is to grow up and be prepared to take the strong meat of detailed biblical truth. And this discussion of Jesus' priesthood has brought us to the point where, as we noted, the longest biblical quotation of the whole letter is found: the promise, in Jeremiah 31.31–34, that God will make a new **covenant** to replace the one he made with Moses.

These quite different phases of the letter, like the different stretches of a river, each have their own character, but it's important to see the way in which each follows on naturally from the previous one, forming one long single argument. To change the image quite drastically: it's a bit like a wedding cake, with each layer carefully positioned on top of the previous one – except that, whereas wedding cakes normally have smaller layers the higher you go, in this letter it's the later layers which get larger and larger. Jesus is the Messiah, God's son, superior to angels and hence to the law; he is the truly human being, and he offers the true 'rest' which goes far beyond what the Israelites were expecting after the **Exodus**.

In fact, as Messiah, he is the true high priest, who has accomplished what the ancient priesthood was never able to.

Now, as a result of all this, we see that in him God has fulfilled one of the most central and vital promises of all: he has established, in Jesus, the new covenant spoken of by Jeremiah. And, just as Psalm 95 continued to be the vital text in chapters 3 and 4, and Psalm 110 from chapter 5 to the middle of chapter 8, so Jeremiah 31 continues to be in the writer's mind, and should be in ours as well, all the way from this point to the end of chapter 10. Many other streams of thought come into the river through this stretch, and we shall take note of them as they do so; but the countryside we are now in is new covenant territory. And the point Hebrews wishes above all to make about the new covenant, as we see in verse 12, is that through it sins have at last been forgiven. With this, the previous covenant, **Temple**, priesthood and all, are 'out of date' and 'about to disappear' (verse 13). This is the most powerful argument yet for the importance of holding on to Jesus instead of going back to the apparent safety of Judaism. If God has established the new thing he had always promised, to go back to the old is foolish as well as disloyal.

HEBREWS 9.1–10

The Old Tabernacle Points Forward to the New

[1]The first tabernacle had, of course, its own regulations for worship, and it contained the earthly sanctuary. [2]A double tent was constructed. In the outer one was the lampstand, the table and the 'bread of the presence'. This is called 'the holy place'. [3]After the second curtain came the inner tent, called 'the holy of holies'. [4]This contained the golden altar, and the ark of the covenant, which was covered completely in gold. In the ark

were the golden urn containing the manna, Aaron's rod that budded and the tablets of the covenant. [5]Above it were the cherubim of glory, which overshadowed the mercy seat. There is much we could say about all this, but now is not the time.

[6]With all these things in place, the priests continually go into the first tabernacle in the ordinary course of their duties. [7]But only the high priest goes into the second tabernacle, once every year, and he always takes blood, which he offers for himself and for the unintentional sins of the people. [8]The holy spirit indicates by this that, as long as the original tabernacle is still standing, the way is not yet open into the sanctuary.

[9]This is a picture, so to speak, of the present age. During this period, gifts and sacrifices are offered which have no power to perfect the conscience of those who come to worship. [10]They only deal with foods and drinks and various kinds of washings. These are regulations for the ordering of human life until the appointed time, the moment when everything will be put into proper order.

The taxi driver was resigned to things being this way for a long time. 'Yes,' he said, 'we've just got to put up with it. Boston will be a great city if they ever get it finished.'

We were stuck in what seemed like an impenetrable traffic jam, going from Logan Airport, out by the Atlantic ocean, to the apartment we had rented in Cambridge, Massachusetts, just inland from Boston itself. One of the largest construction projects ever was taking place right in our path, designed to create a whole new road system which would enable traffic to flow smoothly not only between the airport and the city but also between other towns to the north and south.

I realized at that moment – it had never occurred to me before – that for the entire duration of such a project, in this case several years if not decades, alternative arrangements had to be made to enable the traffic to get through, as well as it could, while the building was in process. When a sculptor is carving a statue, she doesn't have to make arrangements for other people to do different things with the same block of wood or stone. But when you redesign a major part of a city, ordinary life has to go on. People have to get to work. In addition to the eventual plan, therefore – the great design in the mind of the planners and somewhere no doubt in a model under a glass case in City Hall – there have to exist all sorts of preparatory and intermediate plans. While the work is going on, they will need to build extra temporary roads going this way and that, which they will then demolish when the final stage is complete. No doubt this work, too, subdivides into several stages. People like me, living there for just a few months, only ever knew the temporary stage. I never saw the final plan, even as a model or a map.

The main point to which Hebrews now comes – in one sense, this is the very heart of the letter – is that God has all along had a master plan for how the world would be put to rights. He has envisaged from the beginning the way in which the wickedness and frailty of his human creatures would be dealt with, so that the entire world, like the city of Boston in the minds of the planners, could be 'put into proper order' (verse 10). But, for all sorts of reasons which theologians and philosophers explore but which ordinary worshippers, like ordinary drivers in a city, may only be dimly aware of, this cannot be done all at once. Temporary arrangements have to be made to keep things flowing, to regulate ongoing human life, until the appointed time.

The present section of the letter all comes under the heading formed by the previous section, in which the writer quoted Jeremiah 31.31–34 in full, focusing on the fact that what has come about through Jesus the **Messiah** is the long-awaited 'new **covenant**', the new bond between God and his people through which, at last, sins would be properly dealt with and forgiveness not only promised but accomplished. But what has all this talk of the tabernacle and its furniture got to do with that new covenant? Why has he launched into this detailed description of the double tent which the Israelites made in the wilderness and the different things the **priests** were commanded to do in it?

The clue comes in verse 9. The double tent – with its outer part where the priests come and go, and its inner part where only the **high priest** goes – is a picture, a '**parable**' or allegory, of the two 'ages', the two periods of time, within the long purposes of God. No wonder the writer warned a few chapters ago that he had some things to say which would make them all think a bit harder. Let's take it carefully, step by step.

The double structure of the tabernacle in the wilderness, reflected then in the structure of the **Temple** in Jerusalem, meant that most things happened in the first tent (or, in the case of the Temple, the outer court). Once a year, at the climactic moment on the Day of Atonement, the high priest would go into the inner tabernacle, the holy of holies, in order to present the blood of the sin-offering. That is the two-stage picture to hold in mind.

All right, says the writer, let's take this double structure as a model. The **present age** – the period of time right up to the coming of the Messiah – was simply the time of temporary arrangements (and the temporary arrangements included, confusingly, the entire tabernacle or Temple itself!). Don't make the mistake of thinking that this whole system, elaborate and well constructed though it is, is what God has in mind as the final scheme. That would be like a visitor to Boston mistaking the complicated temporary road layout for the final one.

As he makes this basic point, which he will elaborate further in the passages that follow, we sense that he could have said much, much more. Verse 5 is the sort of thing you say when you're giving a lecture and realize that, though there is much fascinating material you could include at this point, there isn't time for it, or perhaps that the students aren't ready for that level of complexity. We shall never know what this writer might have said about the altar, the ark, the urn, the cherubim and all the rest. Some of the other incidental things he says – like the comment about the high priest offering blood for the 'unintentional' sins of the people – will be explained in more detail later on. But let us at least get our minds round his central theme. What has happened in Jesus is that, to return once more to my opening illustration, the main road from one side of the city to the other has now been opened. Some of the temporary roadways are still standing, but you shouldn't mistake them for the real thing. His readers need to know that they can now travel by the main highway straight into the heart of the city. If anyone tells them they should still use the old roads, the answer is not that those old roads were a bad thing, but that they were a good thing whose purpose has now been accomplished. In Jesus the great high priest, God has put things into proper order at last. He has thus established the new covenant, in which sins have been fully and finally dealt with.

HEBREWS 9.11–14

The Sacrifice of the Messiah

[11]But when the Messiah arrived as high priest of the good things that were coming, he entered through the greater and much superior tabernacle, not made with hands (that is, not of the present creation), [12]and not with the blood of goats and calves but with his own blood. He entered, once and for all,

into the holy place, accomplishing a redemption that lasts for ever.

¹³If the blood of bulls and goats, you see, and the sprinkled ashes of a heifer, make people holy (in the sense of purifying their bodies) when they had been unclean, ¹⁴how much more will the blood of the Messiah, who offered himself to God through the eternal spirit as a spotless sacrifice, cleanse our conscience from dead works to serve the living God!

The first time we moved house we could hardly believe our luck. We went from a basement flat to a house above ground. The flat had been damp, even to the point of growing fungus on the walls; the house was warm and snug. We had had no garden at the flat; now we had a small lawn, with flowerbeds and a beautiful tree. Moving was hard work, but it was worth it in every way. Everything was better.

The writer to the Hebrews continues to explain that the new **covenant** has arrived in Jesus. His underlying emphasis is that his readers should continue to enjoy their membership in Jesus' people, whatever the cost, rather than think of going back to their previous home, their native Judaism. Here he makes the point to which the previous section was building up: that, with the **Messiah**'s arrival, the promised new world has been opened up, and it is better in every way.

It is better, first, in terms of the tabernacle which he has entered. The **priests** under the old system went daily into the **Temple**, the successor of the wilderness tabernacle; the **high priest** went annually into its inner sanctum, the holy of holies. But all along, as Hebrews explained at the start of chapter 8, this tabernacle or Temple was a secondary thing, a temporary substitute for the reality which God had in mind all along, the ultimate sanctuary or tabernacle which was the very presence of God himself in the **heavenly** realms. We may perhaps find it difficult to think of this heavenly sanctuary as an actual building, and of course that's the point; the building on earth, 'made with hands' (verse 11), is simply a signpost to the reality. The reality is that God dwells in light and holiness which would dazzle us to bits. We can only come near to him if someone, like the high priest in the Temple, goes in ahead to present the tokens of our purification, to certify that we have been passed as fit to enter.

The second way in which the new covenant is better than the old, then, is that the Messiah has presented before God, not the blood of regular animal **sacrifices**, but his own blood. This is perhaps the most striking, indeed shocking, idea in the whole letter. At almost no point in the voluminous Jewish literature from the Bible through to the Jewish writings contemporary with the New Testament, and indeed beyond, does anybody suggest that *human* sacrifice might be a good thing – still less that the Messiah himself would become such a sacrifice. Apart from the powerful and deeply mysterious passage in Isaiah 53.10, which speaks of the sacrificial death of God's servant, the closest that Judaism comes to such an idea is the story of Abraham sacrificing Isaac at Mount Moriah (Genesis 22), a story which played a considerable role in Jewish thinking at this time, and which Hebrews will refer to in 11.17–18; but the point there, of course, was that God stopped Abraham actually killing Isaac. The sacrifice didn't happen. Nor, of course, was there ever a suggestion that a high priest would have to become, simultaneously, *both* the priest who offered the sacrifice *and* the sacrifice itself. The idea would have been laughable if it hadn't, almost certainly, appeared blasphemous.

The writer is here leading us closer and closer to the heart of the deep mystery which sacrifice involves. It seems to have at least three elements. First, there is the sense of humans offering to God something valuable and pure as a sign of their grateful offering of their whole lives to him and his service. Second, there is a sense of the life of the sacrificial animal, symbolized by the blood, being poured out in death as a sign that, though our lives are indeed forfeit because of our wickedness and impurity, God will rescue us by providing a life-given-in-death instead of ours. Third, there is a sense that through these two signs our present state of uncleanness can be washed away so that we can start afresh, cleansed and fit for God's service. It is hard to say how much of this was present to the minds of ancient Israelites as they came to worship. But symbolism often communicates to people even if their conscious minds don't bring it into articulate thought.

When you take these three elements as something like the meaning of ancient Israelite sacrifice, you begin to see the ways in which the Messiah's death could take their place as a better, and indeed final, once-for-all, sacrifice. As the representative human being (see chapter 2), Jesus' offering of his own life to God, laying it down obediently in death, stands as the offering of the whole of humanity. His life-given-in-death, similarly, functions on our behalf; he died, therefore we need not do so. Third, whereas the ancient animal sacrifices functioned as a way of purifying the outward lives of worshippers (who might have become 'unclean' either through physical pollution or through the effects of their own sin), the self-offering of Jesus, as the representative Messiah and as the true high priest, have a cleansing effect that goes far, far deeper.

This brings us to the third and last way in which his sacrifice is 'better'. It reaches to the depths of the personality. Just as Jesus has gone into the very heart of the presence of God, not simply into a man-made building with an inner chamber but into the place where God lives in light and holiness, so the effects of his sacrifice are to be felt not only in the outer lives of his people, in terms of restoration to fellowship or being made 'clean' again in a bodily sense, but in the inward depths, the 'holy of holies' at the core of each individual person, the place where we really are who we are. Hebrews will speak several more times about the 'conscience' of worshippers (see 9.14; 10.2; 10.22; 13.18). Each time, the writer is stressing the fact that under the new covenant there is a purification available which goes to the centre of things.

In particular, this purification can wash us clean from 'dead works' so that we can 'serve the living God' (verse 14). As we saw earlier (6.1), the 'dead works' refer both to pagan practices from which one would turn in **repentance** on becoming a Christian and to the regular round of Jewish ritual which, though good and God-given in itself, could never actually accomplish what was required, namely, dealing with sin and death. Now the living God, the God whom Israel had always worshipped but whose saving plan was still in the preliminary stage, had revealed once and for all the way into his presence, the way in consequence by which his people could serve him gladly and joyfully without the slightest shadow or stain on their consciences.

Many Christian people, still today, forget that they are called to that kind of exuberant and joyful service, free from any motivation caused by guilt or fear. Why do you suppose that such a liberating and healing **message** would be so hard to believe and remember? Why would we not want to move house to something that is better in every way?

HEBREWS 9.15–22

The Purpose of the Blood

[15]For this reason, Jesus is the mediator of the new covenant. The purpose was that those who are called should receive the

promised inheritance of the age to come, since a death has occurred which redeems them from transgressions committed under the first covenant.

¹⁶Where there is a covenant, you see, it is vital to establish the death of the one who made it. ¹⁷A covenanted will only takes effect after death; it has no validity during the lifetime of the one who made it. ¹⁸That's why even the first covenant was not inaugurated without blood. ¹⁹For when every commandment had been read out to the people by Moses, he took the blood of calves and goats, with water and scarlet wool and hyssop, and sprinkled the book itself and all the people, ²⁰saying, 'This is the blood of the covenant which God has made with you.' ²¹He then sprinkled the tabernacle, and all the vessels used in worship, with blood. ²²In fact, more or less everything is purified with blood according to the law; there's no pardon without bloodshed!

To some, this passage is one of the most central in scripture; to others, it's one of the most shocking. After the twentieth century, in which more human blood was spilled through war, torture and miscellaneous violence than in all previous centuries put together, many people have reacted angrily against what they see as a kind of primitive theology. No pardon without bloodshed, they say? The very idea is barbaric.

Well, we shouldn't be too quick to hurl charges of barbarism around the place. Our modern society tolerates, even fosters, so many things that previous generations, and other civilizations today, would consider barbaric (atom bombs, abortion as a method of birth control, anti-personnel land mines . . . and that's just a few beginning with 'a'), that we are hardly in a position to glance at something deep and mysterious in a different culture and declare, high-handedly, that it's primitive, barbaric or bizarre. But let's at least be sure we've understood what's going on in this passage.

As we saw earlier in the chapter, the point of **sacrifice** within the Old Testament system, where very detailed regulations were laid down for it, was a combination of at least three things: humans offering to God something which represented their own true selves, the outpouring of **life** to signify dealing with sin, and the effects of both of these in the cleansing or purifying of the worshipper. Now we go a stage further, even more mysteriously, into the heart of the second of these. Somehow, it seems, the blood of the sacrificial animals was pointing forward to a deeper truth still: that at the heart of the sacrificial system there lies the self-giving love of God himself.

What the passage is basically saying, as verse 15 indicates, is that Jesus is indeed the one through whom there comes into being the 'new **covenant**' spoken of in chapter 8. Chapters 9 and 10, as we saw, are basically an extended exploration of this 'new covenant', and particularly of its promise that sins will finally be forgiven in a way they hadn't fully been under the previous covenant. But now the writer introduces a new idea. A covenant can only come into force on the death of the person who made it.

This seems odd in itself, until we realize that the word for 'covenant' is the same Greek word as 'will' in the legal sense. Before somebody dies, they make a 'will' or 'covenant', disposing of their assets as they please. This legal document is binding, but (obviously) it does not come into effect until the death of the testator has been established. With great daring, it seems, the writer now proposes that the new covenant itself only comes into force after the relevant death . . . which means, of course, the death of Jesus.

For this argument to work, verses 18–22 must be taken to mean that the blood of the sacrificial animals, through which the first covenant made through Moses came into being, was somehow a representation of the self-giving love of God. He emphasizes that everything to do with that first covenant – the book itself in which it was written, the people with whom it was made, the tabernacle where the sacrifices would thereafter take place and the vessels of various sorts that were to be used in the regular worship – everything had to be sprinkled with the blood. The blood of the animals was saying, in relation to every possible aspect of the Israelites' regular relationship with God, 'All this happens because I love you enough to give my own self, my own life, for you.' The animals are not just, it seems, representing the people who come to worship; they stand as a gift from God to his people, with their death (symbolized by the poured-out lifeblood) as a sign of God's own self-sacrificial love.

Nobody in that world came near to drawing the conclusion that God would himself become human and would actually offer his own life, literally shedding his own blood, so that all these signs and symbols would become a reality. This is such a huge idea, so powerful in its impact, that many, even many Christians, shrink away from it in horror or disgust. I sometimes wonder if this passage, with this idea central to it, is the reason why Hebrews, though such a magnificent and deeply encouraging book, seems to be ignored or marginalized in many churches. Yet the idea of God shedding his blood, powerfully paradoxical though it is, is central to other New Testament texts as well, such as Paul's speech to the Ephesian elders (Acts 20.28). Until something like this has been said, we have not done justice to the meaning of Jesus' death as seen by the very earliest Christians.

That, then, is why the last sentence, striking as it is, is so important. It isn't trying to establish a general principle, as though whenever any pardoning needed doing there had to be some blood involved. It is stating how things were in the God-given regulations for the first tabernacle and the consecration of its furniture and vessels. Everything had to be purified with blood, signifying the purification and pardon that was needed for sinful human beings. There was to be no loophole, no point in the entire system at which anyone could suppose that their worship, their buildings, their liturgy or they themselves could do without the self-giving love of God. No room was left for human pride. Everything had to be dependent on the grace of God. And if that was true in the system of the old covenant, which pointed forwards as a signpost to the new one, how much more is it true now that Jesus has embodied in his own life and death, his own bloodshed, the loving pardon which God always longed to give.

HEBREWS 9.23–28

The Messiah's Work in the Heavenly Sanctuary

[23]That's why it was necessary for the copies of the heavenly objects to be purified in this way, while the heavenly things themselves require better sacrifices than these. [24]For the Messiah did not enter into a sanctuary made by human hands, the copy and pattern of the heavenly one, but into the heavenly one itself, where he now appears in God's presence on our behalf.

[25]Nor did he intend to offer himself over and over again, in the same way as the high priest goes into the sanctuary year after year with blood that isn't his own. [26]Had that been the case, he would have had to suffer repeatedly since the foundation of the world. Instead, he has appeared once, at the close of the ages, to put away sin by the sacrifice of his own self.

[27]Furthermore, just as it is laid down that humans have to die once, and after that comes judgment, [28]so the Messiah, having been offered once and for all to take away the sins of many, will appear a second time. This will no longer have anything to do with sin. It will be in order to save those who are eagerly awaiting him.

'It was such a great day,' she said. 'I'd really like to do it all over again!'

We were looking at the photographs two weeks after the wedding. All their friends and relatives had been there. The sun had shone. The music was magnificent. The reception had been grand, the speeches good, the late-night party enormous fun. The sort of day that comes, to most of us, once in a life-time, if that.

That, of course, is the point. You don't get married every year, every month, every week. The reason you have such a big party is precisely that this is supposed to happen once and once only. (Of course, the world being what it is, with marriages ending through death or divorce, people do some-times have more than one wedding; but the point still holds, in that you don't get married again and again *to the same person.*) Some events mean what they mean precisely because they are one-off. To repeat them would be to show that you hadn't understood, or that somehow it hadn't worked the first time.

This is what Hebrews is insisting, in this chapter and the next one, when it stresses that the death of Jesus happened 'once and for all' (verses 25–26 and 28, picking up 9.12, and in 10.10). It was precisely something that happened once. It could not and should not be repeated. This is central to the way in which Jesus' **sacrifice** is 'better' than those which were regularly offered by the **priests** in the **Temple**, under the regulations of the old **covenant**.

To introduce this, the writer explains that the **heaven**ly sanctuary, like the earthly one, needed purifying, albeit in a superior fashion. This (like much in the present section) is bound to seem puzzling at first glance. Why should the heav-enly sanctuary need to be purified? What could have been wrong with it?

The answer, it seems, is that there wasn't anything wrong with the heavenly sanctuary itself, but that it needed to be made ready for the arrival of people with whom there had been a very great deal wrong – namely, sinful human beings. How could we possibly come into the very presence of the holy God? We couldn't, of course. But, since that's what we are promised will happen, and since Jesus' sacrifice is the way by which it happens, the writer can speak with perfect sense of Jesus purifying the heavenly sanctuary itself, so that when other human beings are welcomed into it they will find, as the Israelites found in the earthly sanctuary, that everything there, too, bears the mark of God's self-giving love. Jesus has gone right into God's very presence.

Verse 24 speaks, literally, of Jesus appearing 'before God's face'. This was a powerful idea in Jewish tradition: seeing God's face was such a devastatingly awesome experience that even the angels which flanked God's presence had to veil their faces (Isaiah 6.2). Now Jesus has gone in to see the father's face, and has done so on our behalf, against the day when we will share that glorious vision and do so unafraid, because of the blood which has purified us through and through.

This brings us to the central statement of the passage, in which the writer makes the sharp contrast between the again-and-again nature of the old sacrifices and the once-for-all nature of the one Jesus offered. He has in mind in particular not so much the regular daily sacrifices which the ordinary priests offered in the Temple, but the great annual Day of Atonement in which the **high priest** would go, just that one time, into the holy of holies. What Jesus has done, he says, is both like that and unlike that. There may be many signposts to your destination, but only one destination; in the same way, there were many Days of Atonement from the early times of Israelite worship right through to the writer's own day, but there was only one Day on which Jesus died. There would never be another one.

This was the moment the writer refers to as 'the close of the ages' (verse 26). Actually, the word I've translated 'close' is a bit more complicated than that. Literally, it refers to something which joins on to something else, and so makes one or both of them complete. That is exactly what Hebrews means at this point, though we don't have an English word that catches the flavour of it all in one. The old **age** and all that went with it was coming to an end; the events of Jesus' life and death were bringing the old dispensation, the old covenant, to its fulfilment, its completion, its goal, its close. At the same moment, the new age, long promised and awaited, was now dawning. And the central characteristic of that new age, as Jeremiah had indicated, was that sins would now be forgiven once and for all.

Jews of the first century would have been familiar with how the ritual of the Day of Atonement worked. After the preliminaries had been completed, the high priest would go into the holy of holies with the sacrificial blood, to make the annual atonement for the people. He would then re-emerge, both to declare that the sign of forgiveness had once again been performed, and to set about the work of dealing with the problems that remained in the community, the practical outworking of the ritual.

The writer has this picture in mind, too. Jesus, the true high priest, has gone into the heavenly sanctuary and will reappear. At the moment his followers are eagerly awaiting that great day. (Together with 10.37, this is Hebrews' clearest statement of the 'second coming'; it shows that the writer and his readers both took it for granted.) This time, however, it would not be to do anything further in relation to sin. No more work of atonement would be necessary. When Jesus reappears, it will be with one aim: to save those who are waiting for him, to transform them (as Paul says in Philippians 3.20–21) so that they become the people God wants them to be as citizens of his new creation.

HEBREWS 10.1–10

The Stopping of the Sacrifices

[1]The law, you see, possesses a shadow of the good things that are coming, not the actual form of the things themselves. Thus it is unable to make worshippers perfect through the annual round of the same sacrifices which are continually being offered. [2]If the worshippers really had been purified once and for all, they would no longer have sin on their consciences – so they would have stopped offering sacrifices, wouldn't they? [3]But, as it is, the sacrifices serve as a regular annual reminder of sins, [4]since it's impossible for the blood of bulls and goats to take sins away.

[5]That's why, when the Messiah comes into the world, this is what he says:

You don't want sacrifices and offerings;
Instead, you've given me a body.
[6]You didn't like burnt offerings and sin offerings.
[7]Then I said, 'Look! Here I am!
This is what it says about me in the scroll, the book:
I've come, O God, to do your will.'

[8]When he says, earlier, 'you don't want, and you don't like, sacrifices, offerings, burnt offerings and sin offerings' (all of which are offered in accordance with the law), [9]then he says, 'Look! I've come to do your will!' He takes away the first so that he can establish the second. [10]And it's by that 'will' that we have been sanctified through the offering of the body of Jesus the Messiah, once for all.

Last year we had one vacation inside another one. We had gone off for three weeks to a quiet, peaceful spot to recover after several months of hectic and unrelenting work and activity. But while we were there the opportunity came for us to take a short trip to a lovely town on the south coast of Ireland. We were only there for four days, but when we came back to resume our main vacation we felt as though we had been away for a month. It provided an extra depth to the holiday and meant that when we finally came back to work we were all the more refreshed and rested.

Putting one idea inside another one, when you're writing a book, may seem a complicated thing to do, but like putting one vacation inside another one it may increase the power of the whole experience. Here Hebrews does exactly this, and it's important to see what's going on in case we miss the full picture and then wonder how the details fit. In this passage, and on to the end of verse 18, the author is still expounding the passage from Jeremiah 31 which he quoted in chapter 8; that is to say, he is still explaining the way in which the death of Jesus has brought about the true forgiveness of sins, to which the **Temple sacrifices** pointed but which they could never finally accomplish. And he is explaining how this achievement of Jesus therefore brings about the new **covenant** in which the forgiveness of sins was the central promise. He doesn't mention Jeremiah 31 explicitly in the present passage, but we should never forget that he is still intending to explain how it has been fulfilled.

Now, however, he launches into another biblical exposition within that larger one. He picks yet another Psalm, this time Psalm 40.6–8, which explains, he says, the way in which the voluntary offering of a human being, coming to do the will of God, is the real thing which God wanted, the real thing for which all the sacrifices and offerings of the Temple cult were simply signposts, and somewhat inadequate ones at that. Or, changing the picture just a little, they were like shadows of the reality, not the reality itself – shadows cast by the bright light coming from God's future.

At this point, and at one or two other moments in this letter, many readers have wondered if perhaps the writer is using ideas that had been made famous by the philosopher Plato. In particular, the idea of something being a 'shadow' rather than a 'real form' sounds like his well-known picture of the Cave, in which people who haven't yet been enlightened think they're looking at reality but are in fact only looking at shadows cast by objects that remain out of sight.

This appearance, though, is superficial. The contrast the writer is making is not, like Plato, the contrast between physical objects and non-physical ideas, or 'forms'. As verse 1 insists, it is the contrast between the *present* and the *future* realities. Jesus, who has gone ahead of us into God's future reality, will reappear when that future reality bursts into the present for the whole world. And he himself was and remains a thoroughly physical human being.

What was wrong with the sacrifices and offerings of the old covenant, says Hebrews, wasn't that they were physical, 'earthly' in that sense. Jesus' own sacrifice was just as earthly, just as much a matter of physical reality, as the animal sacrifices in the Temple. That always was part of the truth of Christianity, however scandalous it may seem to tender-minded Platonists in the ancient or the modern world. What was wrong was that the old sacrifices needed to be done over and over again, thus demonstrating that they hadn't really dealt with the problem. If I have to take my car back to the mechanic every week with the same problem, that's a fair indication that he hasn't succeeded in fixing it.

In particular, as we saw in chapter 9, the regular round of

sacrifices under the old covenant could never address the problem of sin and guilt in the *consciences* of the worshippers (verse 2). They could, after their own fashion, effect purification from outward impurities, such as you might contract, under the Mosaic **law**, through such unavoidable actions as coming into contact with a corpse. They could assure people of continuing membership in Israel despite their sins. But they could never achieve the deep cleansing, the healing of memories and imaginations, that the blood of Jesus has achieved and can achieve. They couldn't, in that sense, 'take sins away', restoring sinful human beings to an actual condition in which their consciences had been rinsed clean, enabling them to stand boldly and gladly in the presence of God.

As so often in this letter, the writer draws attention to something written under the old dispensation which points forward, inescapably, towards the new. This time it is Psalm 40, which speaks from the heart of the Old Testament, surrounded with the rules for the daily sacrifice, of the fact that, for all that those sacrifices were commanded by God, they are not what he really wants. This isn't the only Old Testament passage which says this sort of thing; compare, for instance, 1 Samuel 15.22, Isaiah 1.10–17 or Hosea 6.6 (quoted by Jesus in Matthew 9.13 and 12.7). Together these passages form telling reminders, just as we saw with Psalm 95 in chapters 3 and 4 and Psalm 110 in chapters 5–8, and as we are seeing with Jeremiah 31 in the present section, that the Old Testament, the earlier dispensation, points away from itself to something else, something better, something which God desires and which he is planning to accomplish.

At the heart of this new thing, this better dispensation, is the voluntary, obedient self-offering of the son. Over against the sacrifices, he has come to do God's will (verses 7, 9). This means, as the writer has been saying one way or another all through the letter, that the law, for all its majesty, for all that God deliberately gave it to Israel in the first place, cannot be regarded as the final word. What Jesus the **Messiah** has done, once and for all, comes both as the crown and completion of God's previous purposes and as the new reality which takes their place.

And, again as he has been emphasizing all through, and will shortly draw to a head, this means that the readers would be mad to think of going back, as though for safety, to the old system. It might get them out of a little local difficulty in their immediate situation. But it would be like running for safety into a house which was about to fall down. The old system itself pointed forward to the new, declaring itself ultimately redundant. To agree with Psalm 40 is not, therefore, to say that there is anything wrong with the Old Testament, or the system it put in place. That system itself declared itself to be temporary. Now that the proper replacement has come, nobody in their right mind would stay with the temporary one, let alone go back to it having once experienced the new, and permanent, dispensation which has come to birth.

HEBREWS 10.11–18

The Finished Achievement of the Messiah

[11]Thus it comes about that every priest stands daily at his duty, offering over and over the same sacrifices, which can never take away sins. [12]But Jesus offered a single sacrifice on behalf of sins, for all time, and then 'sat down at the right hand of God'. [13]From that moment on he is waiting 'until his enemies are made a stool for his feet'. [14]By a single sacrifice, you see, he has made perfect for ever those who are sanctified.

[15]The Holy Spirit bears witness to this too. For, after it is said,

> ¹⁶This is the covenant I will establish with them
> After those days, says the Lord;
> I will give them my laws in their hearts, and will write them
> Upon their minds,

then he adds:

> ¹⁷And I shan't ever remember
> Their sins and all their lawlessness.

¹⁸Where these are put away, there is no longer a sacrifice for sin.

Many of us in the modern world do our work sitting down. I'm sitting at a desk as I write this; I'm aware that my posture isn't perfect, that I'm in danger of getting stiff shoulders, and that if I took more time to walk around, let alone to do more strenuous exercise, I'd probably be fitter and healthier for it. Accountants and lawyers do much of their work sitting down. Business people spend long hours at their desks. Many shop-keepers sit at a till. When we stand up, it's a sign that work is over for the moment and we're off to do something else.

For much of the world, though, and for much of history, the act of sitting down meant that you had finished work, not that you were beginning it. In a world where most working people laboured in the fields or in energetic crafts like building, only a few sat down. Most people stood to work and sat to rest. That is the contrast which Hebrews is making here between the **priests** who (in his day) still served under the old dispensation, offering regular **sacrifices** in the **Temple**, and the position Jesus has now taken after completing his work. They all stand daily at their duties (verse 11); he has finished his work, and now sits at God's right hand (verse 12). He doesn't have to offer his sacrifice any more; he's done it, and it's complete.

110

Before we explore this further, note what the writer is doing. He is coming back one more time to one of his favourite passages, Psalm 110, which he quoted right at the start of the letter (1.13) and expounded in detail (the bit about Melchizedek) in chapters 5–8. Now he returns again (verses 12 and 13) to the verse which he referred to early on, the verse about the **Messiah** sitting at God's right hand until God makes his enemies into his footstool (Psalm 110.1). This, as you will recall, fits neatly with Psalm 8.6, quoted in Hebrews 2.8, about Jesus as the representative human being, 'under whose feet' everything has been put in subjection. We thus have a sense, here in chapter 10, of several strands of thought in the letter as a whole being drawn together and fitting into the eventual big picture the writer has all along been holding in his mind. The picture of Jesus as the Messiah, the truly human being, the great **high priest** after the order of Melchizedek, the one who has offered the perfect sacrifice through which the sin-forgiving new **covenant** has been established at last – all these belong together. The argument of the letter is about Jesus at every point. The result of discovering, with the help of the Old Testament, what Jesus has achieved is to realize that he has fulfilled God's purposes as set out in scripture, so that the only wise place to be is with him, rather than with those who cling to the signposts instead of the reality.

When we look to see where this Jesus is now, and what he's doing, we discover, not that he needs to die over and over again, like the regular repeated sacrifices offered in the Temple; nor, indeed, that he is again and again presenting his sacrifice to the father, as though he needed to do that repeatedly within the **heavenly** sanctuary. It is true, of course, as we saw in 7.25, that the continuing work of Jesus in the heavenly sanctuary is now to 'make intercession for' his people. He is there 'on our behalf' (9.24). But he is no longer at work; no longer sacrificing, or offering his sacrifice. That was done once and for all, and is finished and complete. He has taken his seat, signifying that his principal work is over.

The writer intends that his readers should find this enormously comforting. What Jesus has done, in dying as a sacrifice for us, to procure the complete forgiveness of sins spoken of in Jeremiah, and to establish God's new covenant with us, is complete. It does not need adding to, let alone repeating. To suggest either of these would be to suggest that there was something incomplete, something left undone which Jesus didn't quite manage to do the first time round. When as Christians we look for assurance that we have truly been forgiven, we don't look – or we shouldn't look – at anything we do, at anything the church does, at anything Christian ministers, clergy, priests or whoever do. We look back to the event outside Jerusalem on that dark Friday afternoon, and thank God for what was accomplished fully and finally on our behalf.

This, unfortunately, has become a matter of considerable controversy, and there are many Christians who remain unclear about it. The time when Jesus spoke most strikingly about the 'new covenant' through which sins would be forgiven by the shedding of his blood was of course at the final meal he shared with his **disciples**, the 'last supper' which he commanded his followers to repeat 'in remembrance of me'. This event, and the keeping of this command by Christians ever since (the 'Lord's supper', the 'mass', the '**eucharist**', the 'holy communion'; call it what you like), are enormously important. We shouldn't be surprised that different interpretations have grown up as to what exactly this meal means, and, so to speak, how it works.

One major strand of thought within some churches has seen the meal as itself a sacrifice, and has seen the clergy who conduct the liturgy as 'priests' in the sense of people who offer this sacrifice. There is just a grain of truth in this, since the meal which Jesus commanded us to repeat always takes its meaning from the single sacrifice he offered. From that point of view it is true to say that we are continuing to share in the single sacrificial event, like the priests or people in the Temple eating the meat after the animal had been slaughtered. But this isn't all that has usually been meant when people have seen the eucharist as a sacrifice. The present passage rules out entirely any further notions down this line, particularly any suggestion that the sacrifice of Jesus is somehow repeated at each service.

What then does Paul mean when he says that, as often as we eat the bread and drink the cup, we 'show forth the Lord's death' until he comes (1 Corinthians 11.26)? He means that the meal itself *proclaims*, or announces, the single, past, unrepeatable event, not that it somehow re-enacts it. The only time anything is said in the New Testament about re-crucifying the **son of God**, it is mentioned as a dire warning of something nobody in their right mind would wish to do (6.6).

There is, of course, more to be said on this subject. I don't pretend to have covered it with any completeness. But we should be aware, since these questions are still raised from time to time, that at this, the climactic moment of one of the major letters in the New Testament, it is emphasized that the sacrifice of Jesus was a single moment in history which accomplished forgiveness, and is not to be repeated. Christianity is not a religion that imagines itself going round and round in a circle, coming back to the same point. It is not a religious *system* like that at all. It is about events that move forwards, in a historical sequence, from a beginning, to a development, to a climax, to the results of that climax. Part of being a Christian is to know where you belong within that story, and to celebrate what it means: that God's dealing with our sins, and establishing his new covenant with us, have been achieved once and for all.

HEBREWS 10.19–25

So – Come to Worship!

¹⁹So then, my brothers and sisters, we have boldness to go into the sanctuary through the blood of Jesus. ²⁰He has inaugurated a brand new, living path through the curtain (that is, his earthly body). ²¹We have a high priest who is over God's house. ²²So let us therefore come to worship, with a true heart, in complete assurance of faith, with our hearts sprinkled clean from an evil conscience and our bodies washed with pure water.

²³Let us hold on tightly to our confession of hope, without being diverted; the one who announced the message to us is trustworthy! ²⁴Let us, as well, stir up one another's minds to energetic effort in love and good works. ²⁵We mustn't do what some people have got into the habit of doing, neglecting to meet together. Instead, we must encourage one another, and all the more as you can see the great day coming closer.

I watched as my mother came in from shopping, carrying several bulging bags. She called me to help get the rest from the car. I couldn't think why she'd bought so much food, but I fetched and carried and unloaded as best I could. Then I remembered all the telephone calls the previous week. Normally she wouldn't make more than two or three calls a day, but there had been perhaps a dozen or two. Then, that evening, she enlisted my help again in tidying the main front rooms of the house, and in polishing a table here and some cutlery there. I was surprised, but didn't think more of it; I was no doubt living in my own small world, as children do.

But then, the following afternoon, the doorbell began to ring and one person after another came into the house. It was a party! All the shopping, phone calls and polishing had been getting things ready for a celebration. Friends and neighbours were invited. Everything was prepared. Now I saw where it had all been going.

Hebrews has now, if I can put it like this, done the shopping, made the telephone calls and polished the silver. At last the invitation goes out: come to the party! Verse 22 is the primary reason we've come all this way – collecting key passages from scripture, marshalling arguments here and there, calling up ideas and images familiar and unfamiliar, shaping and polishing the exposition of Jesus as God's son, the truly human one, the great **high priest**, the mediator of the new **covenant**. Now we see where it's all been going. 'Let's come to worship!' Verses 19–21 lay out, in summary form, everything we have seen so far: our boldness of access into God's presence through Jesus' blood, which takes us on a new, living path into the innermost shrine through the work of our high priest. The result of it all can hardly be anything but an invitation to draw near; and 'drawing near' is almost a technical term, in this context, for 'coming to worship'.

But not just any worship, and not in any old state of mind. Verse 22 continues by telling us four things about the condition *we* should be in as a result of all that has been said.

First, we should have 'a true heart'. This looks back to the promise in Jeremiah 31.33, quoted in verse 16 above and in 8.10, that God will place his laws in our hearts and write them in our minds. Something happens to people when the new covenant opens up to include them within it – something involving the heart. They become truly human beings, from the inside out. It starts with the heart and works its way into the rest of the personality, thinking, behaviour and all.

Second, we must have 'complete assurance of **faith**'. Faith isn't something you can just drum up like that by your own efforts. It's what comes when you are looking hard at the object of faith, namely Jesus – or, if you like, God seen in the light of, and in the face of, Jesus. The whole letter has been about Jesus, and about who we are as a result of who he is and what he's done. Thinking that through, and holding firmly on to it, produces the complete assurance Hebrews is talking about.

Third, and applying the first two points a bit deeper, we must have 'our hearts sprinkled clean from an evil conscience'. As we noted earlier, this was the great effect of the **sacrifice** of Jesus (9.14). Most people, most of the time, have something which hangs heavy on their hearts, something they've done or said which they wish they hadn't, something which haunts them and makes them afraid of being found out. How wonderful to know that the sacrifice of Jesus, and the 'sprinkled blood' which results from it, has the power, as we accept it in faith and trust, to wash every stain from the conscience, so that we can come to God without any shadow falling across our relationship.

Fourth, the writer speaks of 'our bodies being washed with pure water'. This is presumably a reference to **baptism** (see 6.2), seen as the sign of entry into God's renewed people, though this letter never makes the point any more explicit than this.

So, then, we are to come to worship God – not just in private, though private worship and prayer is enormously important, but in public as well. The danger of people thinking they could be Christians all by themselves was, it seems, present in the early church just as today, and verse 25 warns against it. This may well not be due to people not realizing what a corporate thing Christianity was and is, nor yet because they were lazy or didn't much like the other Christians in their locality, but because, when there was a threat of persecution (as will become clear later in this chapter) it's much easier to escape notice if you avoid meeting together with other worshippers. Much safer just not to turn up.

There's no place for that, declares Hebrews. Every Christian needs the encouragement of every other Christian. Everyone who comes through the door of the place of worship, whether it be a house in a back street or a great cathedral in a public square, is a real encouragement to everyone else who is there. This is part of the way, along with an actual word of encouragement when necessary, in which we can 'stir one another up' to work hard at the central actions of Christian living, 'love and good works' (a deliberately broad phrase to cover all sorts of activities). And we need this encouragement all the more, as verse 25 concludes, as we believe that we are drawing closer to the great day when, with Jesus' reappearance (9.28), God will complete his work of new creation (12.26–28).

In particular, then, our worship must be accompanied by a firm grip on 'our confession of hope', the hope that looks forward eagerly to what God is finally going to do for us, the hope that we 'confess' as part of our badge of identity. When questions about it arise in our minds, the answer is not to try to think up clever answers ourselves, but to trust in the one who has promised it to us, that is, the God we have learned to recognize in Jesus. He is utterly trustworthy – a theme we find echoed, like so much in this letter, in Paul (1 Corinthians 10.13; 1 Thessalonians 5.24; and other places).

The party is all prepared; the invitations have gone out; the silver is polished; the host stands waiting at the door. Are you ready to accept the invitation and come in?

HEBREWS 10.26–31

Warning of Judgment

[26]For if we sin deliberately and knowingly after having received the knowledge of the truth, there is no further sacrifice for sin. [27]Instead, there is a fearful prospect of judgment, and a hungry fire which will consume the opponents. [28]If someone sets aside the law of Moses, they are to be 'put to death on the testimony of two or three witnesses', with no pity. [29]How much worse punishment, do you think, will be appropriate for people who trample the son of God underfoot, and dishonour the blood of the covenant by which they were sanctified, and scorn the spirit of grace? [30]We know the one who said, 'Vengeance belongs to me; I will pay everyone back,' and again, 'The Lord will judge his people.' [31]It's a terrifying thing to fall into the hands of the living God.

It was said of the Roman emperor Gaius Caligula, who went mad and did all sorts of bizarre things, that he took to inventing new laws, and having them carved in small letters on tablets and then placed high up on walls, too high for people to read them. This then gave him an excuse to punish anyone he wanted for not keeping them. They hadn't been able to see them, but ignorance wasn't accepted as an excuse. Imperial edicts had to be obeyed.

The sheer brutal irrationality of such a practice alerts us to something which is true in many more reasonable codes of law: that people who genuinely don't know the law, and break it, have a good excuse. There are times, of course, when ignorance doesn't count. You can hardly imagine a murderer being let off because he or she hadn't realized there was a law against killing people. Sometimes ignorance is wilful, or even culpable; but at other times it holds good as a genuine excuse. I didn't know there was a law in Montreal forbidding you to park your

118

car with a wheel on the footpath, like people do in England to keep narrow roads clear. When I parked like that, the day after we arrived, the policeman grudgingly accepted my explanation and didn't give me a fine.

Ancient Judaism had very clear rules about sins that had been committed in ignorance: they could and should be atoned for. The same was true, if anything even more so, for 'unwilling' sins, something someone knew was wrong and did by sheer accident, without intending to. You can see this dramatically acted out in Acts 23.1–5, when Paul rebukes the **high priest**, is himself rebuked for doing so, and responds that he hadn't realized the person addressing him actually was the high priest. Here his offence is both ignorant and unwilling; he didn't know Ananias was high priest, and he had had no intention of speaking roughly to a high priest should he meet one. As any law student will tell you, to prove a crime there has to be evidence both that the person actually did the deed and that he or she had what is called *mens rea*, a guilty mind; in other words, that they had intended to do it. It hadn't been an accident.

In the ancient Jewish codes of laws and **sacrifices**, it was made very clear that the sin-offering, the central sacrifice dealing with sin, was specifically to cover sins that were committed either ignorantly or unwillingly. (The key passages are found in Leviticus 4, Numbers 15, and elsewhere in the same books.) If people sinned deliberately, knowing that something was wrong and choosing to do it none the less, there was no sacrifice prescibed for them; such a person was, in the old phrase, to be 'cut off from among the people', in other words, put to death. There was no place, especially among the nomadic and endangered wandering Israelites envisaged by the **law**, for people who deliberately and knowingly flouted the law by which Israel was both defined and defended.

All this background is in mind as Hebrews launches into the most fearsome warning in the New Testament (apart from some on the lips of Jesus himself). The writer is not content with issuing an invitation to come boldly into God's presence in worship, as in the previous section. He realizes, and wants his readers to realize it too, that the alternative is to go back to a place where there is no promise of new **covenant** blessing. Someone who has heard the **gospel** of Jesus the **Messiah**, and has come into fellowship with the people who hold it fast and live by it, and who then turns away and declares that it's all rubbish and he or she doesn't want anything to do with it – such a person, says Hebrews, is trampling God's son underfoot, treating the covenant blood as though it were meaningless, and despising the **spirit** of God through whom comes saving grace.

The question of who precisely such warnings are aimed at is one which bothered the early church from the second and third century onwards, and ought still to concern us today. Some saw it as referring to anyone who, at any point after **baptism**, committed any serious sin. That's why, in the third and fourth centuries in particular, many prominent church attenders put off baptism until the last possible moment – either before death, or, if they were called to ministry, before ordination! They were frightened lest, by subsequent sinning of whatever kind, they might forfeit their entire salvation. Others read it more in the light of what happened when persecution arose. Such passages as this, it was thought, applied principally to people who, under threat of physical violence or death, were prepared to blaspheme against Jesus and revile him. We in our day tend to react in the opposite way. We are so unused to thinking of judgment at all, or of God as in any way wanting to be angry with anyone, that we bend over backwards to downplay warnings like this one and suppose that they only apply in the most extreme cases.

We are probably as greatly deceived, in this respect, as were those in earlier centuries who treated these passages as a warning not so much against sinning as against baptism. It is absolutely basic to both Judaism and Christianity that there will come a time when the living God, the creator, will bring his just and wise rule to bear fully and finally on the world. On that day, as unanimous early tradition insists, those who wilfully stand out against his rule, live a life which scorns the standards which emerge in creation itself and in God's good intention for it, and spurn all attempts at reformation or renewal, will face a punishment of destruction. The images of fire and vengeance – they are only images, but that doesn't mean the reality is any the less fearful – are as frequent in the New Testament, if not more so, as they are in the Old. If there is no place in God's world of justice and mercy for someone who has systematically ordered their life so as to become an embodiment of injustice and malice, then there must come a point where – unless God is going to declare that human choices were just a game and didn't matter after all – God endorses the choices that his human creatures have made. I know, of course, that there are other views held on these matters today, but this seems to me the one which comes closest to what we find in the New Testament.

This passage, then, is a warning about a more specific danger: that someone who has come close to Christian **faith**, and perhaps shared in the life of Christian worship, will then turn round and publicly deny it all. As we noted when looking at 6.1–8, this seems to relate to a quite specific situation of persecution, coming from the direction of non-Christian Judaism, directed (as that of Saul of Tarsus had been) against fellow Jews who were embracing Jesus as Messiah. This will become clearer, once more, as the present chapter proceeds.

But the passage remains as a warning to us as well. If we have got as far at least as reading Hebrews, and trying to see what it might mean for us, we should be all the more eager that there will never come a time when we might give in to the temptation to declare that the whole thing was worthless. The living God, to whom everyone will render account (4.13), is neither to be trifled with nor presumed upon. It was after all a nineteenth-century cynic, not a Christian believer, who said, 'God will pardon me; that's his job.'

HEBREWS 10.32–39

Suffering in Hope

[32]But remember the earlier times! When you were first enlightened, you went through great struggles and suffering. [33]Sometimes you were exposed to public reproach and physical abuse. Sometimes you stood alongside people who were being treated in that way. [34]You even shared the sufferings of those who were imprisoned. When people looted your property, you actually welcomed it joyfully, because you knew that you had a better possession, a lasting one.

[35]So don't throw away your confidence. It carries a great reward. [36]What you need is patience, you see; then, when you've done what God wants, you will receive the promise.

[37]For in just a little while from now,
The Coming One will come, and won't delay;
[38]But my righteous one will live by faith;
And if he hesitates, my soul will not delight in him.

[39]We are not among the hesitators, who are destroyed! We are people of faith, and our lives will be kept safe.

The prophet saw his world crumbling all around him.

He had watched and prayed and warned the people of what would happen if they didn't turn away from their evil ways. He had hoped that some at least would listen, and that the nation as a whole would gradually be brought round to hear and obey. He had waited and watched and hoped.

And feared. Because he knew what the result might be if they didn't. And he was right. Here they came now: a great enemy, fierce and strong, swift as a leopard, menacing as wolves, laughing at opposition, sweeping all before them. Why didn't God act and stop them? Why did he let wicked pagans like this have their way in the world, worshipping their own military might and scooping up whole nations the way fish are gathered in a net?

The prophet is Habakkuk, seeing the people of Babylon sweeping through the ancient Near East, with vulnerable Israel in their path. He realizes that there is no escape. This, it seems, is what God has decreed. And he finds himself called to a different ministry from what he might have expected as a prophet: summoning people simply to wait, to go on praising God even if everything goes wrong (Habakkuk 3.17–18).

In the middle of it all he has a word, like a little motto, for those who remain faithful, who cling on to the God of Israel even when Israel as a nation seems to be drowning before the pagan onslaught. He contrasts the faithful with those who think they can manage by themselves. 'Look at the proud,' he says. 'Their **spirit** is not right in them. The righteous one, however, shall live by **faith**.'

This saying, made famous by Paul's quoting it in Romans 1.17 and Galatians 3.11, emerges here (verse 38) as well. Clearly it was a well-known text in early Christianity. What Habakkuk seems to have meant was that, when everything all around seemed to be turning upside down and inside out, God's true people would hold on and last the course. Faith was what would matter – God's faithfulness to them, and their answering faithfulness to God (the word 'faith' can mean 'faithfulness' in both Hebrew and Greek). The New Testament writers seem to have latched on to the sentence in Habakkuk not least because they believed that the time of trouble for Israel that had begun with the Babylonian invasion had continued, more or less, right through to their own day; and that now, with the coming of the **Messiah**, God was at last making the way through to the new age in which salvation, rescue and deliverance would come to birth.

Hebrews picks up, as well, the previous verse from Habakkuk (2.3): 'It will surely come, it will not delay.' One might suppose that a time-lag of several hundred years would count as a 'delay'; but the point here in Hebrews 10.37 is that, with the coming of the Messiah, the devastating judgment on the one hand, and the rescue from it on the other, are not far off. If (as may well have been the case) the writer lived to see the awful war between the Jews and the Romans, from AD 66 to 70, culminating in the destruction of Jerusalem itself, I think he would have said, 'Yes: that's what I was talking about.' The judgment on Jerusalem (the centre from which persecution had come against those Jews, such as the readers of this letter, who had hailed Jesus as Messiah), could not but be seen as deliverance by those who had undergone the trials spoken of in verses 32–34.

These verses, in fact, give us a clearer indication than almost anywhere else in the letter of the situation which the readers were confronting. Right from the start they had faced terrible times, just like the Christians in Acts 8 or 1 Thessalonians 2. Indeed, the readers of this letter may include some of those very people, or others who had become Christians at the same time; after all, Paul tells us that he had himself been a persecutor of the church (Galatians 1.13 and elsewhere), and that was in the very early days; he himself was then persecuted by his own fellow Jews, as he describes graphically in 2 Corinthians 11. We don't have to look too far, alas, to see contemporary examples of the same thing. Wherever a regime exists which claims absolute power and regards Christian faith and witness as a threat, Christians will come under attack, as we saw with Eastern European Communism in the cold war years, and have seen again with the situation in China and in many Muslim countries. Many Christian readers today know exactly what it's like to suffer public ridicule and physical abuse, to stand alongside those who suffer it, and to find their property being looted and the authorities looking on and doing nothing.

The writer insists, though, that such horrible and frightening moments are to be seen – and, he says, were seen by those early Christians – as themselves a sign of hope. The outrageous lawlessness of plundering other people's property with apparent sanction from the authorities is a pointer to the fact that, though we still live in the evil **present age**, there is coming a new age in which God will give his people a 'better possession' (another use of 'better', which as we saw is one of Hebrews' favourite words). This steers us towards the great picture of the next chapter, in which the writer will draw our attention to the way in which the heroes of Old Testament faith were looking forward to the new world that God would make, in which they would obtain the true inheritance.

Once again, then, his argument, now being rounded off before the final main section of the letter in chapters 11 and 12, returns to the theme of confident hope and patience. The troubles you're going through at the moment, he says, are just what you should expect, granted the fact that the promised new age has already broken in to the present time through Jesus himself – or, if you like, that Jesus has gone on ahead of us into God's future world, and is already there on our behalf – and that we are therefore out of tune with the present world because we are in tune with the future one. Once you realize that, you have every possible motive to hold on in faith, not to hesitate and waver (verse 39). Those who hesitate or shrink back are in danger, as he said in the previous passage, of losing everything. Those who hold on in faith, as Jesus himself had promised, will gain their lives.

HEBREWS 11.1–6

What Faith Really Means

[1]What then is faith? It is what gives assurance to our hopes; it is what gives us conviction about things we can't see. [2]It is what the men and women of old were famous for. [3]It is by faith that we understand that the worlds were formed by God's word; in other words, that the visible world was not made from visible things.

[4]It was by faith that Abel offered a better sacrifice to God than Cain. That earned him the testimony that he was in the right, since God himself bore witness in relation to his gifts. Through faith, he still speaks, even though he's dead. [5]It was by faith that Enoch was taken up so that he wouldn't see death; nobody could find him, because God took him up. Before he was taken up, you see, it had been said of him that 'he had pleased God'. [6]And without faith it's impossible to please God; for those who come to worship God must believe that he really does exist, and that he rewards those who seek him.

I had thought we were alone on the hillside. It had been misty for some of our walk, and at other times sharp little squalls of rain had spat in our faces. But we had kept going, knowing there would be some difficult climbing later on (a rocky crag, likely to be icy at this time of year) but hoping we could get through.

We reached a small plateau, and as we did so the sky cleared for a moment. As we looked around, we noticed quite a large party some way ahead of us. They must have been going at least a couple of hours longer than us, since they had already come to the difficult bit, and appeared to have negotiated it successfully. In fact, the last in the line were near the top of the crag, their red jackets standing out against the snow and ice.

I took out the binoculars to have a closer look. As I brought them into focus, there was a sparkle of light from where the climbers were. Sure enough: ice-axes. They had discovered they needed them to get up the crag. Just as well we had brought ours. Now we knew, looking ahead to the others, what we would be facing, what we would need to cope with it – and the fact that it was possible. They seemed, particularly those who'd already made it up the crag, to be enjoying it.

Hebrews has now reached a plateau from which there is an excellent view of those who have gone on before. Looking at them, the readers can discover for themselves what is up ahead, what they will need to cope with it, and the fact that when they get there themselves there will be a great welcome. The ice-axe which will be all-important in their onward journey is **faith**; the journey will take them all the way to the heavenly city, the new Jerusalem; and the great company that has gone on ahead is the long list of heroes and heroines of the faith, as set out in the Old Testament and subsequent Jewish writings.

Hebrews 11 thus offers two things which go together: on the one hand, a description of 'faith' itself, the key asset which the readers will need (as the letter has said several times already by now); on the other hand, a brief history of God's people, particularly the key figures in the early period, and especially Abraham and Moses. The story then continues in the next chapter, coming all the way to the writer's own time: it reaches its climax with Jesus in 12.2, and then urges the readers to live within the story for themselves (12.4–17), before declaring what the goal of the journey is (12.18–24) and of what will happen at the end (12.25–29). Chapters 11 and 12, taken together, thus tell the story from creation (11.3) to new creation (12.28), from **covenant** (11.8–29) to new covenant (12.24). It remains, all through, the story of faith.

Faith, for Hebrews, is always closely linked to hope. Faith is looking at God and trusting him for everything, while hope is looking at the future and trusting God for it. As we see in verse 1, Hebrews actually defines faith in relation to hope: it's one thing to have a hope, but when you have faith underneath it gives it assurance. I may hope for a better world, for a new bodily **life** beyond the grave; but unless I believe in the God who raised Jesus, my hope may degenerate into mere optimism. I may have a general sense that there are unseen realities around me, perhaps even some kind of personal force for good with whom I should have some sort of a relationship; but unless I believe in the God we know in Jesus, this sense of unseen things will lack conviction. Assurance and conviction were strikingly evident in the people of faith listed in the rest of the chapter; verses 1 and 2 thus offer a double introduction to the double theme that is now to unfold.

Before we launch on the list of faithful people, though, Hebrews takes us back to the beginning, to creation itself. God spoke, and things came into existence, according to Genesis 1 and passages like Psalm 33.6, 9. Nothing existed before; at God's **word** creation sprang to life. (The second half of verse 3 is difficult to translate. Some people think it means that the things you *can* see came into existence out of things you *can't*; in other words, that at creation God was making invisible things visible rather than creating everything out of absolutely nothing at all. I prefer it the way I've translated it above.) It takes faith to see this: faith in God the creator, which is at the root of all authentic Jewish and Christian faith, and at the root, as well, of all Jewish and Christian belief in both judgment (God is the creator, therefore he takes responsibility for putting the world back to rights) and **resurrection** (God loves the physical world he's made, therefore he intends to remake human beings as even more gloriously physical than they are at the moment).

That's enough deep theology for the moment, we can almost hear our author saying as he steps back from what might otherwise have been a complex discussion. Let's bring some characters on stage, and watch what they do. The first two he calls, from Genesis 4 and Genesis 5 respectively, are Abel, the first murder victim, and Enoch, the first person (the other being Elijah) to be taken straight to **heaven** without experiencing death in the ordinary way. Both, however, are puzzling at first sight.

Abel and his brother Cain both brought **sacrifices** to the Lord, according to Genesis 4.3–4. But, while the text declares that Abel brought some of the most valuable lambs he possessed, it merely says that Cain brought some of the produce of his field. Thus, when the offerings were presented, Abel's turned out to be better than Cain's, and God accepted it – which precipitated Cain's anger and his murder of Abel. But the point here (this becomes clear as the chapter progresses) is that God accepted Abel, and will reward his faith through and out the other side of death. Though he is dead, the account of his faith is still a powerful witness to us so much later.

Enoch became a popular figure in Jewish writing of the last few centuries before Jesus, and for some while after. His strange apparent escaping of death seemed to lend him a special aura and mystique. Books were written as though by him, 'prophesying' events many centuries hence (in other words, in the time of the actual writers). But Hebrews turns away from such speculations and simply insists on what Genesis 5.24 says about Enoch (amplified, perhaps, by Wisdom 4.10): he 'pleased God'. That's a powerful thing to say about anyone, but again our writer simply anchors it to the point he wants to insist on: without faith, you can't begin to please God. As we said earlier, you may have a general sense that there is a supreme divine being, and you may even have a suspicion that this being wants people to search for him. But unless you have faith, unless you really believe that God exists and that he does indeed want people to seek him, and will reward them lavishly when they do, you can't actually begin to worship him.

This launches us into the main list of heroes and heroines of faith, which occupies the rest of the chapter. But already we find ourselves challenged by the faith which looks at creation and celebrates the creator, which looks at death and sees the promise of new life beyond, which looks God in the face and, trusting him, builds on that trust a life which honours and pleases him.

HEBREWS 11.7–12

Faith and the Future: Noah, Abraham, Sarah

[7]It was by faith that Noah, who had been warned by God about things that were not yet seen, took the warning seriously and built an ark to save his household. He thus put the rest of the world in the wrong, and became heir to the righteous standing which accords with faith.

[8]It was by faith that Abraham, when God called him, obeyed and went out to a place where he was to receive an inheritance.

Off he went, not knowing where he was going. ⁹It was by faith that he stayed in the promised land as a stranger, living in tents with Isaac and Jacob, who were joint-heirs of the same promise. ¹⁰He was looking ahead, you see, to the city which has foundations, the city of which God is the designer and builder.

¹¹It was by faith that Sarah herself, who was barren, received power to conceive a child even when long past the right age, since she considered that God, who had promised, was trustworthy. ¹²Thus it came about that from one man, and him more or less dead, there was born a family as many as the stars of heaven in number, as uncountable as the sand on the seashore.

'The starry heaven above us' was one of the two central facts upon which the great philosopher Immanuel Kant based his view of God. (The other was 'the moral law within us'.) From the earliest recorded times, humans have gazed up at the night sky and pondered the mysteries of the universe. Of course, people have drawn strikingly different conclusions from what they have seen. Many older thinkers imagined that the night sky was a dome filled with holes through which light could peep. It took a radical shift to see them as individual, and widely different, sources of light in their own right. Only this last week a newspaper article declared that the Milky Way is much larger than we had previously thought. Some astronomers look at the sky and think of God, of infinity, of mysteries beyond our imagining. Others see primitive forces, driving energy and black holes.

In the Bible – indeed, in Psalm 8, which Hebrews has made good use of in chapter 2 – the starry heavens are sometimes used as a jumping-off point for wonder and contemplation. But perhaps better known is the promise in Genesis 15.5, repeated in 22.17, where it is linked to the parallel promise in 13.16: Abraham's family will be like the stars in heaven in number, or like the sand on the seashore. In other words, they will be beyond counting. The Bible doesn't spend much time attempting to prove God's existence on the basis of the extraordinary world we live in, though it acknowledges that creation bears unspoken witness to its creator. Much more important is to hear the promise which this creator God makes to his people, a promise backed up with illustrations from the natural world in which the wonder and power of creation is present, as it were, to confirm that this God is capable of performing what he has promised.

The **faith** of Abraham and Sarah, which is celebrated in this passage, is faith that the creator God is also the **covenant** God; that the particular promises made to this one family, at a time when they seemed flatly impossible, were backed up by the power which made the world. Verses 1–6 thus stand behind verses 8–12, and give body to the idea of 'faith' which this chapter is all about. It isn't just that Abraham and Sarah thought they heard a strange being speaking to them and decided to believe it, but rather that the God they came to know was the creator God, the absolutely trustworthy one, the one who could give **life** where there was none (verses 11 and 12). This will be further developed in the next section.

Working back from the verses about Sarah, then, we find the promise to Abraham concerning the land. Just as Sarah was called to believe that God would give her a child even though she was elderly and barren, Abraham had been called to believe that God would give him a homeland even though he was a wandering stranger, a nomad with no fixed abode. And, of course, though Abraham and Sarah did indeed have a son, they never came to possess for themselves the land which God promised them. All they had was the cave which Abraham bought as a burial place. For the rest, they were living on God's promise.

That, of course, is what Hebrews wants its readers to learn to do. 'Faith' here is not a general religious attitude to life. It's not simply believing difficult or impossible things for the sake of it, as though simple credulity was itself a virtue. The faith in question, as becomes increasingly clear throughout the chapter, is the faith which hears and believes the promise of God, the assured **word** from the world's creator that he is also the world's redeemer, and that through the strange fortunes of Abraham's family he is working to build . . . the city which is to come.

This city, mentioned here in verse 10 for the first time, suddenly emerges as a main theme in these last chapters of the letter. Here and in verse 16 it is the focal point of the promise about the land; in 12.22 it is the heavenly Jerusalem; in 13.14 it is the future city, contrasted with any city to which one might give allegiance here on earth, and perhaps particularly the earthly Jerusalem itself. What exactly does the writer have in mind?

Jerusalem was of course the holy city, David's ancient capital, the centre of the promised land. But, in some ancient Jewish writings roughly contemporary with the New Testament, there were pointers to a deeper reality, to the belief that God had established a 'true' or heavenly Jerusalem, waiting for the day when **heaven** and earth would be remade (or, as the present letter puts it, 'shaken', so that what is unshakeable may remain). This is picked up in the great description of the new Jerusalem in Revelation 21 and 22, and something of the same idea is assumed here.

The principle seems to be the same as the one we saw in the first part of chapter 9. God promised Abraham the land, and the crowning glory of the land was Jerusalem, where the **Temple** would be built. In the same way, all the promises taken as a whole had a first stage and a final stage. The first stage was the entire history of Israel, from Abraham to the **Messiah**; the final stage would be the establishment of the final city of God, the ultimate master-work of the creator.

The stress on Abraham's faith, and the reference to the promise about the stars of heaven, take us back as I said to Genesis 15. In verse 6 of that chapter we find the verse made famous by Paul's use of it in Romans and Galatians: 'Abraham believed God, and it was reckoned to him as righteousness.' Paul links this with Habakkuk 2.4, 'the righteous shall live by faith', which Hebrews quoted a few moments ago (10.38). We should not be surprised, then, when Hebrews uses very similar language in this passage, though we might be surprised to find that here, unlike in Paul, the subject is Noah (verse 7).

Noah believed in God's promise and warning about what was to come in the future. By taking action on the basis of what God had told him, he demonstrated that he had the same kind of faith as Abel and Enoch on the one hand, and Abraham and Sarah on the other. He thus put the rest of the world in the wrong, and became heir to the righteous status, or standing, which goes with faith. Faith, it now emerges, is not only the assurance of unseen realities, and the backbone of hope, as in verse 1; it is not only the belief that God exists and rewards those who seek him, as in verse 6; it is also the badge that marks people out as members already of God's true people. Precisely because this faith is also hope, their membership, and their inheriting of God's promises, does not yet appear in public. Faith enables this standing, this 'righteousness', to be affirmed in the present time. Hebrews thus agrees more or less exactly with what Paul means by '**justification** by faith', one of the New Testament's most powerful, encouraging and comforting doctrines.

HEBREWS 11.13–22
Faith that Looks Beyond Death

[13]All these people died in faith. They hadn't received the promise, but they had seen it from far off, and had greeted it, and had recognized that they were strangers and wanderers in the land. [14]People who say that sort of thing, you see, make it clear that they are looking for a homeland. [15]Had they been thinking of the place from which they had set out, they would have had plenty of opportunity to go back to it. [16]But as it was they were longing for a better place, a heavenly one. That's why God is not ashamed to be called 'their God', since he has prepared a city for them.

[17]It was by faith that Abraham, when he was put to the test, offered up Isaac; yes, Abraham, who had received the promise, was in the very act of offering up his only son, [18]the one about whom it had been said that 'In Isaac shall your family be named'. [19]He reckoned that God was capable of raising him even from the dead; and, in one sense, he did indeed receive him back from there.

[20]It was by faith that Isaac blessed Jacob and Esau. [21]It was by faith that, when Jacob was dying, he blessed the two sons of Joseph, and 'worshipped, leaning on the top of his staff'. [22]It was by faith that, when Joseph was coming to the end, he spoke about the Exodus of the children of Israel, and gave instructions concerning his own bones.

'Dad, will you walk on ahead just a bit?'

They were going into the middle of town on a Saturday morning. Why would his 14-year-old daughter ask him to walk ahead, rather than beside her as he had been doing?

He meekly obeyed. (Always the best thing to do.) They walked on, some distance apart. After a few minutes she skipped up and rejoined him. Then it came out. Some people she knew from school were walking up the other side of the road. She hadn't wanted them to think that she was doing something so boring, so old-fashioned, so unbearably uncool, as to walk into town beside a middle-aged man, even if he was her father. She made it up to him handsomely later on. But for a moment she'd been ashamed to be thought of as his child. I remember experiencing something similar myself when our car was the most battered one in the school car park on Parents' Day and our son had to make a joke of it to his friends to get round the shame of having parents who couldn't afford a gleaming new machine like everyone else.

Of course, often it's the other way round. There must be many times when parents feel they will die with shame when their friends come round to the house and there, in the main living-room, is a half-dressed teenager slumped across an armchair, listening to loud rock music and drinking cola. And there are many times when the school calls the parents in and makes them blush with tales of what their offspring have been up to. At such a time, it takes great daring as well as love to stand alongside the child in question and not be ashamed to be known as 'their' parents.

This makes it all the more striking when Hebrews declares in verse 16 that God is not ashamed to be called 'their God'. Who are 'they'? Answer: Abraham, Sarah and the others who had continued on their journey, looking for God's promise but never receiving it during their lifetimes. The idea of God being somehow specially related to his chosen people, in an intimate **covenant** bond, is what Jeremiah was talking about in the 'new covenant' passage quoted in 8.8–12, with the focus here particularly on 8.10, which quotes from Jeremiah 31.33: 'I will be *their God*, and they shall be my people.' God is not ashamed to be associated with this strange little nomadic family, to be seen in their company and known as 'their God'. He loves them; he has called them; they believe in him. They trust him. They are taking him at his word, living by his promise, trusting him even through death.

Hebrews thus makes the same kind of move, in relation to the **faith** of the patriarchs and matriarchs, that it had made earlier with the great expositions of scripture. When dealing with Psalm 95, Psalm 110 and Jeremiah 31, the point being made was that the Old Testament points beyond itself. If you go back to the scriptures of Judaism, Hebrews argues, you will find them pointing forwards to something in the future, something which Judaism, at the turn of the eras, knew it did not contain in itself. Now, in the present passage, the letter demonstrates that the patriarchs must have been looking, not just for a homeland, but for something in the future beyond the present life. They were not content to think that their descendants would inherit the land. They were looking for an inheritance that they, too, would share.

And the point is that God has prepared one for them. We noted in the previous passage that the writer has introduced the idea of the 'city of God', the ultimate dwelling-place in relation to which the promise about the land is just an advance signpost. But what is this city, and where is it?

At this point many readers have been content to say, simply, that the city is in **heaven**, and that this is a way of speaking of the place to which God's people go, in one simple move, after they die. Hebrews does not develop very much its view of the destiny of God's people after death; it does not, for instance, spell out what Paul makes clear, that final **resurrection** is a future stage *after* '**life** after death', a new embodiment following a period of disembodiment (except for those still alive when the Lord returns). Nor does it make clear, what Revelation insists upon in its picture of the 'heavenly Jerusalem', that at the last this new city will come down *from* heaven *to* earth, as part of God's whole project of recreating and so reuniting the entire cosmos. But the emphasis on resurrection which begins in verses 17 and 18, and is continued in verse 35, added to the key passages we shall examine towards the end of chapter 12, incline me to think that the writer has the same sort of thing in mind. He is clear, at least, that until the coming of the **Messiah** none of the men and women of faith from days gone by could be 'made perfect', could have their hopes brought to completion. Even after death, they were still waiting. Having hailed the hope from far off, they were content to stare death in the face and continue to believe. No wonder God is not ashamed to be called 'their God'. They are taking him seriously as the creator, the life-giver, the one who can and will raise the dead.

This explains why the writer goes on in verses 17–19, within the story of Abraham, to the famous chapter (Genesis 22) where Abraham is tested by being asked to **sacrifice** Isaac, the son of whom the promises had spoken (Genesis 21.12, quoted in verse 18). This story was important for various Jewish thinkers who explored the mysterious challenge issued by God to Abraham as a test of more or less blind obedience.

Even a moment's thought about what the incident involved for Abraham, let alone for Isaac, and not forgetting Sarah back home, reveals the extraordinary level of faith God was demanding. And, though the planned sacrifice was called off at the last minute, when God realized that Abraham really did believe and really was obedient, there is a sense, says the writer, in which Abraham did receive Isaac back from the dead. He had already abandoned him to God in heart and mind; now he gained him back once more. This way of reading the story is then filled out by the brief mention of Jacob and Joseph. They too looked beyond their own deaths to a future fulfilment, not just in that their descendants would inherit the land, but in that they, too, would have a part to play in God's eventual purposes.

The picture of faith is thus being filled out from one angle after another, as the chapter follows the story of Israel's beginnings. It remains a constant challenge to us as we read it today. Will we continue to trust God for his promises, even if there is little sign within our own lifetime of their being fulfilled? Have we thought through, and firmly grasped, the nature of the 'heavenly city' which we are promised, towards which all earthly cities are at best long-range signposts?

HEBREWS 11.23–31

Faith and the Future: Moses and the Exodus

[23]It was by faith that, when Moses was born, he was hidden for three months by his parents. They saw that the child was beautiful, and they weren't afraid of the king's orders. [24]It was by faith that Moses, when he grew up, refused to be called the son of Pharaoh's daughter, [25]preferring to suffer hardship along with God's people than to enjoy the short-term pleasures of sin. [26]He reckoned that reproach suffered for the Messiah was worth more than all the treasures of Egypt; he was looking ahead to the reward.

[27]It was by faith that he left Egypt, without fear of Pharaoh's anger; he kept the invisible one constantly before his eyes. [28]It was by faith that he kept the Passover and the sprinkling of blood, so that the Destroyer of the firstborn wouldn't touch them. [29]It was by faith that they crossed the Red Sea as though they were on dry ground, while the Egyptians, when they tried to do the same, were drowned. [30]It was by faith that the walls of Jericho fell down after they had been encircled for seven days. [31]It was by faith that the prostitute Rahab was not destroyed along with those who didn't believe; she had welcomed the spies in peace.

The young man came from a wealthy family. His father was a well-respected figure in the community. Everyone expected the son to follow him in his profession and, like him, attain wealth and noble standing.

But the young man wasn't having any of it. Gripped by a passion for God and a love for the poor – or, as some saw it, by a kind of religious mania – he threw it all off, literally in the case of his fine clothes, walking away naked from his father's angry rebuke before putting on a simple robe and devoting himself to a life of prayer and preaching.

He was, of course, St Francis, whose vocation inspired many others to join him. Astonishingly, within less than ten years, his movement had not only become an 'order' but was divided into different provinces. Within 20 years of his original call to leave all and follow Jesus, he had died. By then there were branches of his order in most of the countries of Europe.

The image of a wealthy young man choosing to leave the lifestyle of the careless rich and devote himself to God's work, not least the care of the poor and oppressed, has powerful resonances with the story of Moses, especially as retold in this passage. Moses, as reported in the early chapters of Exodus, was born when the children of Israel were enslaved in Egypt. His parents rescued him from Pharaoh's edict, according to which all male Israelite children were to be killed; that itself was an act of **faith**, defying the mighty pagan king in the hope of preserving a future for God's people. Then comes the moment which Francis himself might have taken as a model: Moses, having been adopted by Pharaoh's daughter, grew up in the royal court, but clearly knew where he had come from, since he abandoned his life of privilege and set out to liberate the Israelites from their oppressive taskmasters. He initially went about it in the wrong way (see Exodus 2.11–15), but in the end he was placed by God in a position of leadership in which he confronted Pharaoh. Hebrews sees this, interestingly, in terms of an implicit loyalty to the **Messiah** himself (verse 26):

Moses was looking ahead, in the long purposes of God, to the moment when the true King would come, the one through whom Israel and the world would finally be set free from all slavery. Moses, like Abraham and the others, was therefore acting on the kind of faith which Hebrews is highlighting throughout this chapter: the faith in God that looks to the future and knows that God has planned something better than anything we could accomplish for ourselves.

This brings us, in the great founding story of Israel, to the mighty moment of the **Exodus**. Egypt, devastated by plagues, finally permitted the Israelites to leave the country. This itself was a great act of faith on Moses's part; Pharaoh was angry, the army pursued them, but the invisible God (remember verse 1) was before Moses's eyes. In faith, he led the people towards freedom.

The night they left was Passover night. The angel of death, here referred to as 'the Destroyer of the firstborn', struck down the firstborn children of the Egyptians while 'passing over' the Israelite houses. Hebrews had earlier drawn attention to the way in which the sprinkling of blood symbolized and effected redemption under both the old and the new **covenants** (9.13–22). Now the writer looks back beyond the developed sacrificial system to the original moment of redemption, when the Israelites were commanded to sprinkle the blood of the Passover lamb on the doorposts of their houses as a sign. This too was an act of faith, faith in God the redeemer and in his promised future. In the same way, when they found themselves with the Egyptian army behind them and the Red Sea in front of them, Moses trusted God, who led them through the sea on dry ground while leaving their pursuers stranded in the returning waters.

Hebrews has already spoken at some length (in chapters 3 and 4) about the time when the Israelites were wandering in the wilderness, spending 40 years discovering how patient God could be despite their folly and rebellion. Now the story moves rapidly past that long, dusty march, straight to the entry into the promised land. Joshua and his followers encircled the city of Jericho, marching round it seven times and then, on the seventh day, seven times in the day. This was not, of course, a normal military assault. Jericho could have withstood standard forms of attack. It was an act of faith, a dramatized prayer for God to act; and act God did. In the process, one family from the city was rescued, that of the prostitute Rahab, who had given shelter to the Israelite spies when they had come to prepare the way, and had spoken to them of how the fear of Israel's God had fallen on all the inhabitants of the area (Joshua 2.9–13). Her faith (she is mentioned, interestingly, in Matthew 1.5, within the family tree of Jesus himself) gains her a mention, an unlikely heroine alongside the better-known leaders of Israel.

The long catalogue is nearly done, and from here on the pace quickens. But before we allow ourselves to be caught up by that, we should pause and reflect. The writer to the Hebrews is determined that his readers should be thoroughly grounded in the long story to which they have fallen heir. They need to go back to the family album to remind themselves where they had come from. They must think through the sort of faith their forebears had had, and see how the long purposes of God, cherished and believed in the face of impossibilities, dangers and even death itself, are finally fulfilled in the events concerning Jesus, and the new **life** they have as a result. How much more must we, in our day, learn to tell not only the story of Israel but the story of Jesus himself, and of his first followers, carefully and with gratitude, so that our faith and hope may in turn be nourished from the source.

HEBREWS 11.32–40

Faith and the Future: The Great Crowd

[32]What more can I say, then? I've run out of time to tell you about Gideon, Barak, Samson, Jephthah, David, Samuel and the prophets. [33]It was through faith that they overcame kingdoms, put justice into practice, received promises, shut the mouths of lions, [34]quenched the power of fire, escaped the edge of the sword, were strong where they had been weak, became powerful in battle, and sent foreign armies packing. [35]Women received their dead by resurrection; others were tortured, not accepting release, so that they might receive a better resurrection. [36]Others again experienced painful derision and flogging, and even chains and imprisonment; [37]they were stoned, they were sawn in two, they were put to the sword, they went about in sheepskins or goat-hides, they were destitute, they were persecuted, they were ill-treated – [38]the world didn't deserve them! – and they wandered in deserts and mountains, in caves and holes in the ground.

[39]All these people gained a reputation for their faith; but they didn't receive the promise. [40]God was providing something better for us, so that they wouldn't reach perfection without us doing so as well.

It is said that on one occasion the sixteenth-century Spanish mystic Teresa of Avila confronted God about her own suffering, and received the response: 'This is how I deal with my friends.'

'Well,' she replied sharply, 'in that case you shouldn't be surprised if you don't have very many!'

The suffering of the people of God – as a famous book has it, *When Bad Things Happen to Good People* – has long been one of the greatest apparent problems in Judaism and Christianity. Those religions that see the world in terms of an endless cycle, a wheel of Fate, with each life rewarding or punishing you for the good and bad you've done in a previous life, don't have the same problem. Each life attempts to restore the balance left by those that went before. This is reinforced, in (for instance) Hinduism and Buddhism, by the belief that the physical body, and the outward circumstances of life, are largely irrelevant, part of a fantasy world that can't touch the real person who is found deep inside. Sometimes people say things like this intending to express a Christian attitude; but in fact the Christian (and Jewish) view of the body, of physical things and of suffering is very different.

Jewish and Christian theology, in their mainstream forms, always highlight the goodness of the bodily world, both the physical world in general and the human body in particular. Evil exists, and is real and powerful. But evil, in these religious traditions, is a parasite on an essentially good world. This then simply heightens the problem. Why is there not only suffering in the world, but suffering – often terrible, intense and shocking – for people who love and trust God? Some of the greatest minds of the last two centuries have given themselves to puzzling away at this question from a wide variety of religious, theological and philosophical standpoints. The Lisbon earthquake of 1755 gave a huge impetus to such questionings in the eighteenth century. The Jewish Holocaust of the 1940s put the question back on the agenda in a new and horrific form.

Since the present passage offers a long catalogue of people who faced terrifying situations, and in many cases were persecuted to within an inch of their lives if not beyond, it raises all these questions quite acutely. Why should it be like this? What's wrong? Why, if God was at work in the lives of Gideon, Barak, Samson and the rest, and those who were stoned, sawn in two, and so on – why, if God was calling them and was with them, did they have to go through all that?

It's important to begin by saying that there's never a full, or ultimately 'correct', answer to the question 'why' in such circumstances. If you could analyse the situation in each case and explain 'why', you would make things seem not so bad; and part of the point is that they *were* bad, very bad, for those involved. You can't somehow draw the sting of torture and murder by locating them, loftily, on some scale of higher invisible purpose.

But when we have said that, we come to the point the writer is making, here in particular, in his long list of heroes and heroines of the faith. He is now drawing a conclusion from their experience similar to the one he had drawn, again and again, from the Old Testament. The fact that they suffered such things, and that they demonstrated that the world wasn't worthy of them, was a sign both that they believed that God was making a new world in which everything would be better, and that this belief was in fact true. They were out of tune with their times because they were living by **faith** in God's future world while society all around them was living as though the present world was all there was or ever would be; and God was giving them strength to live like that, thus proving the truth of their claim. They were, in their own lives and sufferings, living beacons of hope, pointers to the fact that the God who had made the world was intending to remake it, and that they were the advance guard of that great moment.

As with the **Temple** furniture in 9.5, so here we would love to know what the writer might have said about Gideon, Barak and the rest. It would be fascinating to know, too, which people he had in mind in verses 33 and 34. Some we can pick out (Daniel with his lions, and the three young men in the burning fiery furnace, are the most obvious), while in other cases the categories are somewhat loose and could cover several different candidates. The list in verses 35–38 of those treated brutally gives us some clues, too; Elijah and Elisha both restored children who had died to their mothers, and in the later books of the Maccabees we have a whole family of brothers, together with their mother, who were tortured to death, declaring as they suffered that God would bring them to bodily **resurrection** hereafter. For the rest we cannot so easily identify who is in mind, but that's not the point. The clue comes in verse 38: *the world didn't deserve them*. The world would, no doubt, look and see some apparently very odd people, living what appeared to be an extreme form of asceticism, a counter-cultural lifestyle. From God's point of view, these were the beginning of the new world.

Their faith shines all the more brightly when we realize that they carried on throughout their lives without seeing the story come to its proper conclusion. They didn't, in fact, receive the promise, because it only came true in Jesus the **Messiah** and in the community that formed around him. 'God was providing something better for us' – there's that 'better' word again, so much a favourite of Hebrews – and the result is that they won't reach 'perfection', another big word for Hebrews, 'apart from us'. In other words, the community that is now going to be described, the fellowship of those who follow Jesus, establishes the true beginnings, not merely the advance signs, of the world that God intends to make, the world that is to be, the world in which justice and right will triumph. As we look back at the great crowd who went through so much while looking forward to the reality which we now enjoy, are we not rebuked for sitting so lightly on our privileges and doing so little to show that we are the community in whom what they were hoping for is finally coming true?

HEBREWS 12.1–3

Looking to Jesus

[1]What about us, then? We have such a great cloud of witnesses all around us! What we must do is this: we must put aside each heavy weight, and the sin which gets in the way so easily. We must run the race that lies in front of us, and we must run it patiently. [2]We must look ahead, to Jesus. He is the one who carved out the path for faith, and he's the one who brought it to completion.

He knew that there was joy spread out and waiting for him. That's why he endured the cross, making light of its shame, and has now taken his seat at the right hand of God's throne. [3]He put up with enormous opposition from sinners. Weigh up in your minds just how severe it was; then you won't find yourselves getting weary and worn out.

I went to a school that prided itself on its outdoor pursuits. Set high in the Yorkshire Dales in north-west England, it celebrated its location in several ways, the annual climax being a ten-mile cross-country race over steep, difficult ground. Often as many as eighty or a hundred boys would enter this race, with the purpose for most of us being not to win – we left that to the serious athletes – but to get round in a reasonable time, to forge on through mud and heather until we made it back to the finish in the small town where the school was situated.

The year I ran in the race I came, if I remember rightly, about thirty-fifth; respectable though undistinguished. But the thing I remember most vividly was the final stretch, the last half mile or so. I had trained for the race over the previous weeks, and had been round the actual course several times. I was quite used to the closing stages: here we were, back again, almost at the point of a rest and a bath and a hot drink. But this time it was totally different. I had known there would be spectators, of course, but I hadn't prepared myself for the hundreds of boys, parents and local people from the town who turned out to watch as we all came back, bedraggled but mostly happy, from our hour and a half of hard work. They were cheering, waving flags, clapping and shouting encouragement and congratulations. It went on and on, down the road into the town, increasing as we got to the middle, reaching an extraordinary roar as, with a friend running beside me, I rounded the final bend and came down the road to the finish. All these people! Where had they all come from? And such noise! It felt like being a real celebrity, if only for two minutes.

Several aspects of this climactic passage in Hebrews draw on the image of the Christian pilgrimage as a long-distance race, and the first is, obviously, the 'great cloud of witnesses' all around us. Those who have gone before us, from Abel and Abraham right through to the unnamed heroes and heroines noted at the end of chapter 11, haven't simply disappeared. They are there at the finishing line, cheering us on, surrounding us with encouragement and enthusiasm, willing us to do what they did and finish the course in fine style. The difference is, of course, that in a race the runners are competing against one another, whereas in the journeying of God's people what matters most to each runner is that all the others make it safely home as well.

What must we do to run the race with efficiency and success? The writer continues the athletic imagery to suggest three things in particular.

First, we must get rid of any heavy weights that are slowing us down. Athletes sometimes train carrying heavy packs on their backs, to build up strength and energy against the time when, for the actual race, they will run without any extra weight at all. But far too many Christians try to run the race of Christian pilgrimage while carrying all kinds of heavy baggage – anxieties about trivial concerns, ambitions to use the **gospel** as a means of self-advancement, resentments at other people, secret greed for the bodily appetites, and so on. In particular, it's possible for sin of one sort or another to get in the way and constrict our movement; though some translations speak here of sin 'clinging closely' to us, the word properly means 'obstructing' or 'constricting'. The writer seems to have in mind the danger an athlete might face if the track isn't completely clear – if someone puts a hurdle in the way, or leaves a bench or other object across the path of the runners. That's what sin can be like when Christians tolerate it in their lives or in the community. It gets in the way, it can trip you up, it can seriously damage your chance of completing the course.

The second point is that this race, like the ten-mile run at my school, is a long haul, and you need patience. There are always some runners who really prefer a short sprint; some of them, faced with a ten-mile run, will go far too fast at the start and then be exhausted after two or three miles. Sadly, many of us will know Christians like that too: keen and eager in their early days, they run out of steam by the time they reach mature adulthood, and by the time they're in middle age or older they have either lost all energy for active Christian living or are frantically trying to recapture the zip and sparkle of a now inappropriate teenage-style **faith**. Give me the person, any day, who starts a bit more slowly but who is still there, patiently running the next mile and the next and the next, all those years later.

The third point is to keep your eyes, or at least your imagination (when you're too far away to see!), fixed on the finishing line and on the one who is at the centre of the cloud of witnesses, waiting there to greet you himself. Jesus ran this course before us. In fact, he pioneered the way, opened up the course and brought it to a successful completion. Our task is to follow in his steps. He has made it across the finishing line, and his encouragement, and the thought of his welcome and congratulations at the end, are the central motivation for us to continue in hope, faith and patience.

The rest of the passage invites us to contemplate what exactly Jesus went through on his own patient journey, and to realize that we have mostly had an easy time of it by comparison. He kept his eye on the joy that was waiting for him – the joy of doing his father's will, of bringing his saving purpose to fulfilment – and he put up with the foul torture of crucifixion, a degrading and disgusting as well as excruciating and agonizing death. Now, as a result, he is in the key position of honour at God's right hand, as the writer had celebrated in the earlier chapters of the letter. Hebrews is keenly aware that the readers are in danger of being weary with all that they are facing, day after day, in terms of threats, persecution, intimidation and mockery from their contemporaries, their neighbours and perhaps their former friends. This is like the long, hard haul up a steep and muddy hill in the middle of a long-distance race. They must keep going; they must remind themselves continually of the one who blazed this trail in the first place; they must think how much worse it was for him. That way they will be kept from becoming worn out completely. As so often in the Christian life, *reminding* yourself of *truth*, not trying to conjure up feelings of this or that sort, is the way to keep going in faith and patience.

HEBREWS 12.4–11

Christian Suffering Is God's Discipline

⁴You have been struggling against sin, but your resistance hasn't yet cost you any blood. ⁵And perhaps you have forgotten

the word of exhortation which speaks to you as God's children:

> My child, don't make light of the Lord's rebuke,
> Or grow weary when he takes issue with you;
> ⁶For the Lord disciplines those whom he loves,
> And chastises every child he welcomes.

⁷You must be patient with discipline. God is dealing with you as his sons and daughters. What child is there that the parent doesn't discipline? ⁸If you are left without discipline (we've all had our fair share of it!), you are illegitimate, and not true children. ⁹After all, we had earthly parents who disciplined us, and we respected them; shouldn't we much rather submit ourselves to the father of spirits, and live? ¹⁰Our earthly parents disciplined us for a little while, as they judged best; but when he disciplines us it's for our advantage. It is so that we may share his holiness. ¹¹No discipline seems to bring joy at the time, but only sorrow. Later, though, it produces fruit, the peaceful fruit of righteousness, for those who are trained by it.

Western society is in a turmoil these days about discipline. We have become very aware of the dangers of physical violence at every level. What happens when a child grows up knowing only that authority belongs to the person who can hit the hardest and hurt the most? Such children may very well translate that into their own lives by becoming determined to be the toughest kid in the gang, the one who can get power by being the most violent. Or it may come out in other ways, as people try to bribe or cheat to get around the law of the jungle. We have seen so much of all this that many people now feel it is wrong to discipline children at all, especially in physical ways.

But at the same time we are horribly aware, not least in the big cities of the Western world, how dangerous, to themselves and to others, are children who have never learned limits, have never discovered the meaning of 'No', backed up with appropriate restraints. Spoiled children on the one hand, and ignored children on the other, are a menace and a nuisance to everyone else, and are unlikely to grow up as happy, well-rounded characters, able to sustain a normal adult life. Clearly some kind of discipline, as one aspect of genuine love and care, is vital.

That's the clue, isn't it: as an aspect of love and care. The question of what sort of discipline is appropriate within a loving home relationship will vary from person to person, from family to family, from culture to culture. But if a parent leaves a child without training, without discipline, without checking and correction, we begin to wonder either if they have a problem themselves (maybe they are too busy chasing money or pleasure) or if the relationship with the child is somehow different from what we had thought. Maybe, we think as we watch a careless father, it wasn't his child in the first place, so he can't be bothered to discipline it as he should . . .

That is the point of verse 8. If we are genuinely God's children – and being 'God's sons and daughters' is one of the central pivots of the biblical picture of God's people – then we should expect that God will treat us as a wise parent does, bringing us up with appropriate discipline. The writer traces the roots of this notion in the biblical book of Proverbs, quoting in verse 5 from Proverbs 3.11–12. He might have chosen several other passages from the same book, or similar ones from the Psalms, such as Psalm 94.12–13. Thus, way back in the early history of Israel, this emerged as one interpretation of what was going on when God's people were suffering: the troubles they underwent were supposed to function as discipline. They were allowed in order that Israel might be trained to higher standards of **faith**, hope and obedience. Some of the prophets saw them not just as God permitting evil people to afflict Israel: they were sent from God directly. Thus Amos, for instance, lists all the things which YHWH did to bring Israel back to him (Amos 4.6–11): famine, drought, blight, pestilence, disaster. It didn't work, and the prophet warns that God was now going to take more drastic action. This lies near the heart, too, of the various interpretations the prophets gave to the **exile** in Babylon.

It may come as a shock to many Christians to discover that there lies ahead of them a life in which God, precisely because he is treating us as sons and daughters, will refuse to spoil us or ignore us, will refuse to let us get away for ever with rebellion or folly, with sin or stupidity. He has his ways of alerting his children to the fact that they should either pause and think again, or turn round and go in the opposite direction, or get down on their knees and repent. I had a friend once who had firmly and finally decided not to join the ordained ministry but to become a chartered accountant. Almost at once he was struck down by a strange disease which forced him to stay in bed for a week, by the end of which not only his mind, but also his heart, and the direction of his life to this day, had been changed. I know another friend who, after doing something stupid which he knew to be wrong, found himself the next day faced with a short-term disaster which so exactly mirrored what he had done that he felt not only thoroughly rebuked but also full of admiration for God's accurately directed discipline. Some people may be shocked to think of God being involved in such comparative trivia. All I can say is that I'd rather be in the hands of a father than a distant, faceless, careless bureaucrat.

The truth of verse 11 is offered so that we can cling to it when things are difficult. There is much sorrow in an ordinary human life; sorrow which was, of course, shared by the Man of Sorrows as he identified completely with us, a point Hebrews has already made forcefully (5.7–10). It is possible, even for Christians, to see it all as meaningless, to fret and fume as though everything had gone wrong. Well, things do go wrong, and we mustn't make the mistake of blaming God for everything ('Why did you do this to me?') as though there were no evil forces out there – and even 'in here', within one's own only partly redeemed human heart – which still have the power to create havoc. But again and again, when we find ourselves thwarted or disappointed, opposed or vilified, or even subject to physical abuse and violence, we may in faith be able to hear the gentle and wise voice of the father, urging us to follow him more closely, to trust him more fully, to love him more deeply. As verse 11 indicates, suffering can be the trowel which digs deeply in the soil of our lives, so that the plant of peaceful righteousness – a life of settled commitment to live as God's new **covenant** people – may have its roots deep in the love of God.

HEBREWS 12.12–17

Watch Out for Dangers!

¹²So stop letting your hands go slack, and get some energy into your sagging knees! ¹³Make straight paths for your feet. If you're lame, make sure you get healed instead of being put out of joint. ¹⁴Follow after peace with everyone, and the holiness which is necessary before you can see the Lord. ¹⁵Take good care that nobody lacks God's grace; don't let any 'root of bitterness spring up to cause trouble', defiling many people. ¹⁶No one must be immoral or worldly-minded, like Esau: he sold his birthright for a single meal! ¹⁷You know, don't you, that later on, when he wanted to inherit the blessing, he was

rejected. There was no way he could change either his mind or Isaac's, even though he wept bitterly in trying to do so.

'It was a moment of madness.'

The politician stood shamefully before the press. He had been caught out soliciting for sexual favours in a notorious part of town. His character was in ruins, his reputation in tatters. He would not now get the senior job he had coveted. There was no way back. His only excuse was that for a moment he had taken leave of his senses. Treating that statement at face value (though many doubted it at the time), it seems that one night he had made a disastrously wrong decision and was now bitterly regretting it. Human character and reputation is like a tree; it takes decades to grow, but it can be cut down or burnt to a cinder in a matter of minutes.

Well, politicians do sometimes come back after public disgrace, though in my country they seldom get very far when they try. But the point of the sharp warning in this passage is that it is indeed possible to do things which bring our character crashing down in ruins and to discover that there is no way back. The classic example we are offered here is that of Esau, the older twin brother of Jacob. His story is told in Genesis 26 and 27, and we need to remind ourselves what it's about if we're to see what Hebrews is saying here.

Jacob doesn't exactly come out of the story with his hands clean, but the focus of the story is the folly of Esau. He had been out hunting in the countryside and when he came back home Jacob was cooking a meal. Esau was famished with hunger; Jacob refused to give him food unless he gave him his rights as the firstborn son, in other words, the principal share of the inheritance from their father Isaac. Esau, it seems, happily swore away his birthright in exchange for the food. Short-term relief, long-term misery.

The plot then unwinds: Jacob tricks Isaac into thinking he is Esau and giving him his rich and full blessing. Esau comes in later and begs for a blessing as well, but is refused: Isaac has made Jacob the heir of everything, and he can't go back on it. Esau weeps, but it's all to no avail. He had sworn an oath himself, and was now (albeit through trickery) made to keep it. There was no way back, no space for a change of heart, no way he could change Isaac's mind either. In verse 17, the text literally says 'he did not find a place of **repentance**'. The word for 'repentance' means 'a change of mind' or 'a change of heart', and once we think into the story we see that, though this probably refers to Esau's own desire for a change of mind, it could also refer to his attempt to change what Isaac himself had thought and done.

It's impossible. I once knew of a man who had cheated his employers. Rather than make a public scandal of the matter, the employers offered him a package deal through which, if he agreed to leave at once, he would maintain his good reputation. The man refused, whereupon he was dismissed and the matter became public. Not long afterwards he tried, through influential friends, to put pressure on the employers to restore his reputation, to say by implication at least that he had done nothing wrong. Not surprisingly, the employers refused. He had made the decision. Decisions have consequences. There was no turning back. That's the kind of situation Esau was in.

What sort of situation in the church, then and now, does Hebrews imagine will be parallel to this? From the beginning of verse 15, it looks as though the writer is aware that within every church, every Christian fellowship, there may be some people, whether few or many, who are, as it were, 'passengers'. They are enjoying being where they are; they like the company of Christian people; they feel safe and secure. But they have not done business with God for themselves. They have not sought, and found, his grace, that loving mercy which goes down to the root of their very being and transforms them at the core. Nobody, says the writer, should 'lack God's grace'. Other members of the community must take care at this point, must watch out for one another and make sure that grace reaches everyone.

Because, if people continue to miss out on knowing God's love for themselves, the warning of Deuteronomy 29.18 may come true. Deuteronomy warns that, even within the people of God themselves, there may be 'a root sprouting poisonous and bitter growth'. Sometimes, from within an apparently happy church or fellowship, discontent can arise. It may take the form of doctrinal or ethical disagreement; these can be real enough, but often they can provide a smokescreen for personal agendas. The sign is always the sense of bitterness that accompanies it. Disagreement between wise, praying Christians can take place without bitterness; where that troubling and poisonous bitterness starts to make its presence felt, we should recognize what's going on. When people are outwardly part of the community, but inwardly not completely open to God's love and leading, they are capable of saying and doing things which disgrace themselves and the community. Like Esau, they can have a moment of madness which creates a new situation, and they can't go back.

This warning therefore takes its place alongside those in 6.4–8 and 10.26–31: a warning that to turn back to the ways of the world after tasting at least the fringe benefits of the new **life** may result in a fixed and unalterable condition of heart and mind. According to 6.4, it is impossible to restore such people to repentance; this seems to be what 12.17 is saying as well. We should be cautious about suggesting that someone who genuinely wants to repent of their sin and get right with

God will ever be refused; but we should be equally cautious about imagining that someone who enjoys Christian fellowship but then plays fast and loose with the consequent moral responsibilities will be able to come back in whenever they feel like it. Decisions and actions have consequences.

The opening verses of this passage, then, urge the readers to sort themselves out, to become the sort of people spoken of in one of the great prophetic passages, Isaiah 35. 'Strengthen the weary hands,' says the prophet, 'and make firm the feeble knees!' (35.3). God is doing a new thing in your midst – read the whole of Isaiah 35 and see – and you must stand up and get on with the job. There is no room for spiritual laziness (which often includes an element of physical laziness as well). If something is going lame, don't shrug your shoulders and say, 'Oh well, I can't do anything about it.' Make sure you find healing.

In particular, follow after peace and holiness (verse 14). Peace with all people is a fine ideal; but this writer, like Paul in Romans 12.18, knows it won't always happen. You must *pursue* it, chase after it, do all in your power to accomplish it. And holiness – well, as Hebrews says, this is what's required if you're to stand in the presence of the holy God. Don't let anyone tell you otherwise. And don't lose it all to a moment of madness.

HEBREWS 12.18–24

From Mount Sinai to Mount Sion

[18]You haven't come, after all, to something that can be touched – a blazing fire, darkness, gloom and whirlwind, [19]the sound of a trumpet and a voice speaking words which the hearers begged not to have to listen to any more. [20](They couldn't bear the command that 'if even a beast touches the

mountain, it must be stoned'.) [21]The sight was so terrifying
that even Moses said, 'I'm trembling with fear.'

[22]No: you have come to Mount Sion – to the city of the
living God, the heavenly Jerusalem. You have come to where
thousands and thousands of angels are gathered for a festival;
[23]to the assembly of the firstborn, whose names are written in
heaven. You have come to God the judge of all, to the spirits of
righteous people who have been made perfect, [24]and to Jesus
the mediator of the new covenant, and to the sprinkled blood
which has better words to say than the blood of Abel.

The year we moved to London we gave each of the children a
map of the city and a small guide to the main attractions.

Predictably, each of them became excited over different
things which the city had to offer. One was noting the main
concert halls and opera houses. Another discovered where the
art galleries were. A third made an instant note of the main
shopping streets. And a fourth found out that we would be
living halfway between London's two main cricket grounds . . .

Most great cities have so much to offer in so many different
areas that it's quite bewildering, when you arrive, working out
what to do and where to go. I haven't even mentioned the
great sights – Buckingham Palace, Big Ben, the Tower of
London, the magnificent parks and gardens, and so on. And of
course London has its darker side: poverty and homelessness,
violence and unemployment, vice and drugs and squalor and
dirt. Far be it from me to suggest that there is any direct
parallel between London and the New Jerusalem.

But the parallel holds to this extent: that the city we are
promised (see 11.10, 16), the city of which, according to this
passage, we are *already* citizens, is so full of exciting and welcoming features that we ought to find it bewildering and
overwhelming. The writer lists one thing after another in verses
22–24, and we'll look at them in more detail presently.

The main thing that strikes us about this whole passage, though, is the head-on contrast of this new city, Mount Sion as he calls it, with the other mountain which plays such a key part in the biblical story, namely Mount Sinai. The writer doesn't actually mention the word Sinai in verses 18–21, but it's obvious that this is what he's thinking of. This makes the contrast all the more powerful when he says, in verse 22, 'You have come to – Mount Sion!' Sion (or Zion as it's sometimes spelled) was the central part of Jerusalem, the part captured by David and made first into the royal city and then the site of the great **Temple**. Thus the great theme of the earlier part of Hebrews, that of the true heavenly Temple into which Jesus has gone on our behalf, and into which we are now invited because of what he's done, comes to its great climax in this passage: the new city *is* the new Temple, the place where God lives in glory and invites his people to share his life.

But this isn't, of course, the only theme in the letter which reaches its high point in this passage. We saw, right at the beginning, that Hebrews was making a strong contrast between the **law** and the **gospel**, between Moses and Jesus; not that the law was a bad thing now happily abolished, or that Moses was to be dismissed as an irrelevant or bad teacher, but that the new **covenant** which has been established in and through Jesus is 'better' in every way (verse 24 provides yet another example of this theme). It is what the original covenant had in mind all along.

In the Old Testament itself, the story which began with Abraham, Moses and Mount Sinai reached its glorious conclusion with the entry into the promised land, the establishment of the monarchy and finally the building of the Temple on Mount Sion. Now, Hebrews is saying, take that story as a whole, and see it as the equivalent of Mount Sinai; it is the complete story of the old covenant. You need to come into the promised land (chapters 3 and 4); you need to benefit from the ministry of the true **high priest** (chapters 5, 6 and 7); you need to realize that you are within the new covenant, where the ultimate **sacrifice** has already been made, through which you can approach the very presence of God himself (chapters 8, 9 and 10).

Hebrews paints this contrasting picture in bold, almost lurid colours. Mount Sinai was a terrifying sight, burning like a volcano, dark with clouds, roaring with strong winds. Out of that, worse, came a trumpet blast and then a voice – and such a voice! According to Exodus 19, where this picture is set out in detail, the voice from **heaven** could be heard at the foot of the mountain, frightening the people even more, and warning (this is the point of verse 20) that nobody, not even an animal, should come anywhere near the mountain, so holy was it. At the centre of the contrast between Mount Sinai and Mount Sion, in fact, is the contrast between a holiness which is terrifying and unapproachable and a holiness which is welcoming, cleansing and healing.

At this very point, though, we should be careful not to slip into a common mistake. People often imagine that the contrast between Sinai and Sion, or if you like between the law and the gospel, is that the Mosaic dispensation was about an exclusive sort of holiness and the new covenant is a matter of an inclusiveness which simply lets everybody come as they are. The previous passage (verses 12–17), and indeed the whole of the rest of the letter, shows how misleading that sort of 'inclusivity' would be. The point about Mount Sion, and the living God whose home it is, is not that holiness doesn't matter, but that a new way has been found and accomplished through which the holiness you couldn't attain under the Mosaic law has at last been achieved. Almost every feature of the heavenly city described in verses 22–24 emphasizes the fact that those who live in the city are not those who have simply been told to come as they are, but those in whom the lavish grace of God has worked such cleansing, such transformation, that they now belong as of right, albeit by sheer grace, within the holy city itself.

Look at the detail and see. The angels are gathered in their myriads in the city (verse 22), not now to give the law, as in chapters 1 and 2, but to celebrate the fact that what the law had not been able to do has been accomplished through the **son of God**. The 'firstborn' – with 11.28 in the back of our minds, we should be able to understand this as meaning 'those who have been redeemed by the shed blood' – are assembled there already, awaiting those of us who are coming to share their life and their privilege of having their names written in God's heavenly record. The fact that God is named as 'the judge of all' is not meant, here, to be a fearsome thing. As the Psalms say time after time, the fact that God is the judge of all is something to be celebrated. Everybody, deep down, wants the world to be put to rights. If they don't, we begin to suspect that they want to be able to exploit it to their own advantage, to get away with things and not be brought to account.

Similarly, the '**spirits** of righteous people who have been made perfect' sums up the whole train of thought throughout the letter in which God's intention was to bring people to that full humanity, that 'perfection' or 'completeness' for which sin needed to be dealt with, consciences purified right down to the bottom, and the whole life brought into glad conformity with God's design. Finally, as the crowning glory of the new Jerusalem, we find Jesus, the one through whom the new covenant, the sin-forgiving dispensation, has been established; and we find the blood which calls, not for vengeance as Abel's did (Genesis 4.10), but for the full pardon and cleansing which Hebrews has already described at some length in chapters 9 and 10. It is a dramatic, exhilarating, glorious picture.

But the most striking thing about it is that, according to verse 22, those who now live by **faith** and hope have *already*, in a sense, arrived at this heavenly city. They already belong there; in prayer and worship they are already welcome before God's throne. This leads to the obvious question: does your life of prayer and worship, whether alone or with your fellow believers, carry the sense of joy and excitement that comes bubbling out of these verses? If not, why not?

HEBREWS 12.25–29

The Kingdom that Cannot Be Shaken

[25]Take care that you don't refuse the one who is speaking. For if people didn't escape when they rejected the one who gave them earthly warnings, how much more if we turn away from the one who speaks from heaven! [26]At that point, his voice shook the earth; but now he has issued a promise in the following words: 'One more time I will shake not only the earth but heaven as well.' [27]The phrase 'one more time' shows that the things that are to be shaken (that is, the created things) will be taken away, so that the things that cannot be shaken will remain.

[28]Well, then: we are to receive a kingdom which cannot be shaken! This calls for gratitude! That's how to offer God true and acceptable worship, reverently and with fear. [29]Our God, you see, is a devouring fire.

The first time I stayed in a hotel in Los Angeles, I was startled by the polite little card on the table beside the television. I am quite used to fire regulations, instructions about laundry and advertisements for room service, but this was different. It was headed 'What to Do in Case of an Earthquake'. All I now remember of it is that I was supposed to hide under the table in case the ceiling fell in. Much good that would be, I thought, since I was on the twenty-third floor. But fortunately the night passed without any tremors or wobbles, and the really interesting question – whether there was enough space under the table for someone of my size to fit – went unanswered.

A real earthquake is of course, along with fire and flood, one of the most frightening events anyone can experience. For so much of normal life we take for granted the stability of the earth, the roads and the walls and roofs of the houses we live in. An earthquake faces people not only with sudden and severe physical danger but also with the deeper shock of realizing that, quite literally, the foundations of their world are not as secure as they thought they were. I mentioned the 1755 Lisbon earthquake a few sections ago; it offered a challenge of yet a further dimension, in that people had been accustomed to speak of the created world as being basically a stable, good place where God looked after people's well-being. Suddenly all that was thrown into question, precipitating a flood of books, poems and philosophical musings on what became known as 'natural evil'.

The really worrying thing in the present passage, though, is that the promise of the earth, and **heaven** too, being shaken comes directly from God, as part of his plan to take his creation by the scruff of the neck and make it, at last, what he always intended it would be. The passage looks back, one more time, to the thunderous voice which came to the people from Mount Sinai, making the earth tremble and quake. Despite the contrast between verses 18–21 and 22–24 – or perhaps because of it? – we now find that the quaking earth at Sinai is replaced in the new **covenant** promises, not with a calm, flat transition to God's new world, but with something even more tumultuous: not only an earthquake but also, so to speak, a heavenquake. As Revelation 21 insists, for there to be new heavens and a new earth the present heavens, as well as the present earth, must undergo their own radical change, almost like a death and new birth.

Hebrews uses a different image for this same transition, but the end result is the same. Heaven and earth alike must be 'shaken' in such a way that everything transient, temporary, secondary and second-rate may fall away. Then that which is of the new creation, based on Jesus himself and his **resurrection**, will shine out the more brightly. This new creation will, of course, include all those who belong to the new covenant, and, through them, the new world which God had always promised. That is what Hebrews 11 and 12 have been telling us all along.

This breathtaking promise of God's new world comes to the readers not only as promise, though, but also as warning. If people who refused to listen to Moses found themselves in dire trouble, what will happen if people now refuse to listen to one who is so much greater than Moses? This brings us back full circle, of course, to 2.1–4, and indicates that the writer is at last completing his great argument and drawing together its threads.

As he does so, the central theme he wants to leave us with, before the concluding instructions of chapter 13, is a true picture of God and of ourselves in relation to him (verses 28–29). Not for him the sentimental pictures of God seen as an indulgent parent, someone always there to comfort, never wanting to make too much of a fuss. The true God is not tame, nor does he spoil his children. He is like a fire: the holiness of God, emphasized through the **Temple** ritual, is not undermined by the fact that, in the new covenant, his people are invited into his presence in a new way. To think like that would be to make a radical mistake. It isn't that God has stopped being holy. God hasn't changed a bit. It is, rather, that Jesus has opened a new and living path, through the 'curtain' and right up to him. Only when we remind ourselves of God's holiness do we fully appreciate the significance of what Jesus achieved. It is noticeable that, where thinkers have spoken of God without stressing his all-consuming holiness, the meaning of the cross is downgraded in proportion. Hebrews, in line with the rest of the New Testament, celebrates the accomplishment of Jesus in his sacrificial death precisely because its view of God has not changed from the central Jewish belief we find in the Old Testament. God is the same; or, to put it the other way round, it is the same God who has now, in Jesus, brought his saving plan, set out in the Old Testament, to a triumphant conclusion.

The appropriate response, therefore, is gratitude and worship. I was talking with a friend the other day who had been wrestling with the question of the proper Christian attitude to what we sometimes call 'the good things of life' – food and drink, money and possessions. Knowing perfectly well that these things can become severe temptations if pursued for their own ends, he had often found himself led in the direction of renunciation, setting aside all interest in and claim on them, going the route of asceticism. Now he had come to the conclusion, he said, without wanting to pursue them in an idolatrous fashion, that the proper response to material goods was gratitude. Thanking God for what you have is the way to keep the things of this world in proper perspective. That way, you can never turn them into idols; nor can you make the mistake of supposing that when God made the world he made trash, which we can ignore or sneer at.

If that is so with the present world, with all its ambiguities, how much more ought we to be grateful for the world that is to come, the world that we have been promised as our true inheritance! True gratitude both for the present world and for the world to come is the deepest and truest form of worship, reaching places which the entire sacrificial system never could. When you bow down before the living God and thank him from the bottom of your heart for what he's done and for what he will do, it is as though you are a **priest** in the Temple, offering the purest, most unblemished **sacrifice**. Only much, much more so. That is the privilege of being a follower of Jesus the **Messiah**. That is the **life** to which our fiery God now calls us. The writer was eager that his readers should listen hard to this urgent exhortation. Two thousand years later, we need to do so every bit as much as they did.

HEBREWS 13.1–8

The Practical Life of God's People

[1]Let the family continue to care for one another. [2]Don't forget to be hospitable; by that means, some people have entertained angels without realizing it. [3]Remember people in prison, as though you were in prison with them. When you think of people who are having a difficult time, remember that you too live in a frail body.

[4]Let marriage be honoured by everyone; let the marriage bed remain undefiled. God will judge those who sleep around or commit adultery.

[5]Keep your life free from love of money; be content with what you have. He himself has said, after all, 'I will never, ever, leave you or forsake you.' [6]That's why we can be cheerfully confident, and say, 'The Lord is helping me; I'm not going to be afraid; what can anyone do to me?'

[7]Remember your leaders, who spoke God's word to you. Look carefully at how their lives came to complete fruition, and imitate their faith. [8]Jesus the Messiah is the same, yesterday, today and for ever.

Sex, power, money, suffering. Tomorrow morning's newspaper will be full of it; it's what sells, it's what some people think makes the world go round. Meanwhile, you can look through the newspaper from end to end for a mention of Jesus. There may be one or two hints (perhaps someone copying the Beatles and claiming to be more famous than him!), but he won't dominate the urgent trivia that is pushed at us day by day and week by week.

Yet here, in the closing chapter of one of the great documents of early Christianity, we find sex, power, money, suffering – and Jesus. What's more, he's the one who makes sense of all the rest. He is the same 'yesterday, today and for ever'. The writer wants us to realize that, if your **faith** is firmly rooted in him, none of the forces that blow people off track and into the newspapers need harm you.

What precisely does he mean by speaking of Jesus in this way? And how can this faith sustain and guide us through these choppy seas?

The whole letter has been about the way in which God guided and led his people from the early days of the old **covenant** through to its fulfilment in Jesus, and how he leads his people from the early days of the new covenant, in which his readers were living, through to their own fulfilment in the 'city which is to come'. Yesterday – in other words, in the period of the old covenant – Jesus was the same: Moses, says our writer, 'suffered abuse on behalf of the **Messiah**' (11.26). He is and was the eternal one who has become human, the one through whom the worlds were made (1.2–3; 1.10–12). Never think for a moment that when Jesus appeared this was, in that sense, a different revelation, or a revelation of a different God, to the one the Israelites had known all those years. It was a fresh revelation of the same God; like meeting someone in person who up to this point you had known only through letters and the occasional telephone call.

Jesus is the same 'today'. The writer has already emphasized 'today', especially in chapters 3 and 4, where he expounded Psalm 95. The message of the **gospel** isn't for tomorrow only; you can't put it off and imagine things will be easier when you've finished this task, made these decisions, earned some more money, and settled down. The challenge of Jesus is for today, for this moment, this decision, this difficulty.

And Jesus will be the same 'for ever'. He is the mediator of the new covenant, the one whose personal presence is the central and most important feature of the new Jerusalem (12.24). The one we know by faith in the present is the one we shall know person to person in the fulfilled world, the new world that will emerge after the present one has been 'shaken', according to God's promise (12.26–28). This whole book has been about Jesus, and verse 8 thus draws together the heart of it in a short, pithy epigram, worth learning by heart or pinning up on a wall.

If we get our picture of Jesus right, the huge issues in the other verses will begin to fall into place. First, the practical life of the Christian community must be ordered in such a way that generosity and love – the love, of course, that reflects and continues to embody God's own self-giving love – will be its central features. The family (in other words, the Christian brothers and sisters) must continue to care for one another in practical ways. Mutual affection is vital; financial help for those in need is vital; the word used in verse 1 includes both. And the hospitality which so marked the early Christian community must be extended wherever possible, with the fascinating promise that in opening your front door you never know when an angel is going to walk in. It happened to Abraham in Genesis 18; it can happen to you.

The writer then turns to the darker side of early Christian experience. Prison has been a feature of Christian life from the earliest days. Those at present enjoying freedom must regularly think of, pray for and find ways of helping those who are in prison. This presumably means, in the present context, people who are in prison because of their faith, and working on behalf of persecuted Christians remains a vital task today. But the writer would certainly not have excluded the wider work of caring for those in prison in the modern world, where locking people up is used far more often as a straightforward punishment than it was in the ancient world. There people were often executed, fined or banished for crimes both serious and not so serious.

Then come two rules of thumb about the perennial storm centres, sex and money. Marriage is to be respected and honoured by all, and nobody must try to break into the sexual union of husband and wife. The pagan world of the first century was every bit as sexually promiscuous as the Western world of the twenty-first century, and Christians are called today, as they were then, to stand out, to be deeply counter-cultural, at this point. The writer warns that God will judge those who flout his intention for the gift of sex, using it as a plaything rather than the deep, rich, satisfying bond between husband and wife that it was meant to be. This judgment will not necessarily be confined to the **life** to come. In fact, as thousands of novels, plays and poems bear witness, it is all too frequent that those who degrade themselves and other people by indulging in sex outside its proper context carry bitter regrets and long-lasting emotional scars.

The same is true with money, which first enslaves people and then laughs at them as it fails to provide the happiness it promised. Not that poverty by itself brings happiness, either; let's not have any romantic notions about that. But the *love* of money is the thing to beware of. When you love something or someone, you make sacrifices for them. When you find yourself making a sacrifice of something else in your life, simply so that you can follow where money is beckoning you, regard that as a danger signal.

The second half of verse 5, the cheerful celebration of verse 6, and the advice in verse 7 to consider those who have been your leaders in the **faith**, all undergird this sober and practical advice. Those who trust in God to be with them for ever, to help them and defend them in and through all circumstances, will be far less likely to fall for the temptations of sexual immorality or love of money, both of which so often attack those who are personally insecure. The confident faith of verse 6 is nothing other than the faith which has been celebrated and encouraged throughout the letter. This is the faith which the earliest Christian leaders possessed, and which must now be imitated (verse 7) by readers both ancient and modern.

HEBREWS 13.9–16

Outside the Old City, Seeking the New

⁹Don't let yourselves be carried off by strange teachings of whatever sort. The heart needs to be strengthened by grace, you see, not by rules about what to eat, which don't do any good to those who observe them.

¹⁰We have an altar from which those who minister in the tabernacle are not allowed to eat. ¹¹For the bodies of the animals whose blood is taken into the sanctuary by the high priest as a sin-offering are burned outside the camp. ¹²That's why Jesus too suffered outside the gate, so that he might make the people holy with his own blood. ¹³So, then, let's go out to him, outside the camp, bearing his shame. ¹⁴Here, you see, we have no city that lasts; we are looking for the one that is still to come.

¹⁵Our part, then, is this: to bring, through him, a continual sacrifice of praise to God – that is, mouths that confess his name, and do so fruitfully. ¹⁶Don't neglect to do good, and to

> let 'fellowship' mean what it says. God really enjoys sacrifices of that kind!

I mentioned earlier that I had been reading the diary of a clergyman who had been a prisoner of war from 1940 to 1945. It was both fascinating and frustrating. Fascinating as a first-hand, day-by-day account of the life such people had to endure. Frustrating because the Germans, not unnaturally, wouldn't let people write things in diaries which they thought might be subversive. Just as all letters coming in or going out of the camp had to be screened by censors, so all diaries – and many prisoners kept them – were regularly checked, and would have been confiscated or destroyed if they had been saying anything too explicit about the progress of the war. This was so especially in the last year or two, when the Allies invaded Europe and the prisoners were eager for news, rumours, anything which might tell them how soon they would be liberated.

The result is that quite a few references to current events were written in a sort of code – and I couldn't always crack it. The writer would refer obliquely to air raids by the Allies. He would hint at things he knew about the progress of the war, which other prisoners would have picked up at once but which I, without help, couldn't fathom. In particular, he would refer to prisoners who were attempting to escape the camp. At one point I realized that a reference to chickens and foxes had nothing to do with farmyards, and everything to do with prisoners who had managed to escape and who, he was hoping, would escape the 'foxes' – the guards or soldiers who might recapture or even kill them – and get home safely.

The passage now in front of us is not so oblique as all that, but to understand it we need to put ourselves in the situation it refers to and watch as it begins to make more sense. At this point, we may well be close to glimpsing the actual historical situation of the readers. They are urged to avoid 'strange teachings' consisting in food regulations. They are encouraged not to worry about bearing the reproach which goes with being a follower of Jesus. They are reminded that the city that matters is not the present one but the future one. They are told, once more, about the true '**sacrifices**' which they are to offer, as opposed to the regular animal sacrifices. They are, in other words, being invited to contrast the present Jerusalem with the one that is to come (12.22–24), and to draw the conclusion: you belong in the latter, not the former.

This doesn't by itself prove that the readers were Jewish Christians who were living in Jerusalem. It may be that they were members of a synagogue community which thought of itself, as it were, as a 'little Jerusalem', somewhere else either in Palestine or in the wider **Gentile** world. But the mention of the altar and the sacrifices does imply that they needed to distance themselves from the city and the **Temple** where sacrifices were offered; and in Judaism there was only one such place.

It is quite possible, then, that this somewhat oblique little section is written in the way it is because both writer and readers knew there was an increasingly tense situation brewing up for followers of Jesus in and around Jerusalem itself. They needed to be encouraged to think through the implications of their **faith**, and be prepared to make the clean break that might well become necessary. Whether or not this actually refers to the time when the Jews in Palestine were in revolt against Rome, between AD 66 and 70, it is impossible to tell. There may have been many crises in which Jewish Christians would be suspected of being traitors to the nationalist cause. But certainly that great war, which ended with the destruction of Jerusalem and the Temple, would fit very well.

What the writer has to say is then full of irony. He warns in verse 9 against 'strange teachings' – referring to the Jewish food laws! Somehow, his readers need to see the Jewish laws about what to eat and how to prepare it, which were and are central to the practice of mainstream Judaism, in the same way that most Jews would regard the kind of teaching that was 'strange', in other words, that came from the Gentile world outside. Rules of this sort, he urges, don't do you any good. You need grace in the heart, not a special type of food in the stomach. To see how controversial this would have been, you only have to glance at Mark 7, or indeed Galatians 2.

Then, in verses 10–14, he compares Jesus once more to the sacrificial animals of the sin-offering. This time his aim is not to highlight the achievement of his own sacrifice – he's already done that extensively in chapters 9 and 10 – but to make a parallel between Jesus, who was put to death outside the city, and the animals whose bodies were to be burned outside the camp. (It is possible, in fact, that throughout the letter one of the reasons the writer has been speaking about the tabernacle in the wilderness rather than the Jerusalem Temple is to avoid mentioning too directly the central institution of Judaism, the building and system which Jesus had declared to be under God's judgment.) The point he is making is that the followers of Jesus are to be happy to leave the city and its Temple, even though their fellow Jews will regard them as traitors and heap shame on them.

Nor should they regard themselves as being thereby deprived of the normal access to God, and feasting in his presence, which took place at the Temple. On the contrary. They 'have an altar' at which they can eat (verse 10). This must be a reference to the **heavenly** sanctuary itself, as expounded earlier in the letter, at which they will be allowed not just into the outer courts, as in the Jerusalem Temple, but into the holy

174

of holies itself, since they have themselves been made holy by the blood of Jesus (verse 12). As a result, they are actually *more* privileged than the Jerusalem priesthood ('those who minister in the tabernacle' – again, it seems, a coded reference). Verse 10 insists that those who do not avail themselves of the new **covenant** privileges now available through Jesus are not allowed at this, the ultimate 'altar'. God has established the new covenant, and no promises remain for those who refuse its blessings.

All this makes sense, once more, because the present city is under judgment. What matters is the one that has been promised, the one that is yet to come. As in Galatians 4.25–26, the present Jerusalem (again, not mentioned explicitly) is in a kind of slavery and is under condemnation. Those who belong to Jesus claim membership in the Jerusalem that is yet to come, as in chapters 11 and 12.

The result of it all, again, is glad and uninhibited worship (verses 15–16). This, rather than endless dead animals, is the 'sacrifice' that God really wants. God wants people who will name the name of Jesus, in prayer, worship and testimony, even if it costs them dear. Their witness will bear fruit. And the common life of the Christian community, the life of generous-hearted fellowship, is itself in that sense a 'sacrifice', an act of worship. God is delighted with it. Never allow yourself to get into the way of thinking that, just because nothing you can do can earn his favour, God isn't pleased with what you attempt in his name. Precisely because love cannot be earned or deserved, it is always delighted when it receives answering love. As the final section of the letter will insist, this too is, in any case, the work of his grace.

HEBREWS 13.17–25
The God of Peace Be with You

[17]Obey your leaders; submit to them. They are keeping watch over your lives, you see, as people who will have to give account. Make sure they can do this with joy, not as a burden. That would be of no value to you.

[18]Pray for us! Our conscience is clear; we are quite sure of it. We wish to act appropriately in everything. [19]I beg you especially to do this, so that I may quickly be restored to you.

[20]May the God of peace, who led up from the dead our Lord Jesus, the great shepherd of the sheep, through the blood of the eternal covenant, [21]make you complete in every good work so that you may do his will. May he perform, in you, whatever will be pleasing in his sight, through Jesus the Messiah. Glory for ever and ever be his, Amen!

[22]I beg you, my dear family, bear with this word of exhortation; I've written to you quite briefly, after all. [23]You should know that our brother Timothy has been released. If he comes soon, I will see you and him at the same time.

[24]Greet all your leaders, and all God's people. Those from Italy send you greetings. [25]Grace be with you all.

I was chatting with a friend who had recently become a bishop. He was and is a wonderful man, scholarly, wise, outgoing, full of ideas and devotion and love and goodness. You might have thought any church would be glad to have him as a leader.

'How are you finding it, then?' I asked.

'Trying to be a leader in this church', he replied, 'is like trying to take a cat for a walk!'

Now there are some rare cats who like being taken for walks. Sometimes, as we say, they seem to think they're dogs. But mostly they respond badly to any attempt to suggest that they might like to do this or that. They tend to look slightly offended, and do the opposite. All too often, it seems, Christian

176

people behave in the same way. The present mood of Western society, in which all authority seems suspect, and all power is assumed to corrupt people, gives an extra excuse to people who want to do their own thing rather than submit in any way to what anybody else says.

And yet there are appropriate structures of responsibility within God's church; because, as we find in passage after passage, God regards his people as sheep in need of shepherds. Jesus himself is of course the true shepherd, as Hebrews will say in verse 20; but in John 21, memorably, he called Peter to act as a shepherd over his flock, and he hasn't stopped calling shepherds ever since.

The point, of course, is that shepherds are there to look after the sheep, not to 'rule' them like a dictator, nor to use them for their own advantage, as so many politicians do even in the supposedly free and democratic world. In so far as the shepherds are doing their job, it is in the sheep's best interests to follow where they lead. This isn't 'patronizing' (the familiar charge today); it's common sense. Every Christian, every congregation, needs to recognize that God does indeed call people to lead, teach, instruct and warn the flock, and that it is better all round if this task can be done joyfully.

Verses 18 and 19, and 22 and 23, give small indications once more of the situation of both the writer and the readers. Verse 19, which sounds similar to what Paul says in Philemon 22, may indicate that the writer is himself in prison, though nothing so far in the letter has led us to suspect that. Maybe he is simply engaged in difficult work which prevents him from coming to them at the moment. The sudden mention of Timothy in verse 23, and of his being 'released', links this letter to Paul's world, but frustratingly doesn't help us get much further with identifying its writer or place of origin. The mention of 'those from Italy' in verse 24 doesn't necessarily mean that the writer was in Italy at the time; it might easily indicate that there was a small community, wherever he was, who had come from Italy – consisting perhaps of those, like the people mentioned in Acts 18.2, who had been expelled from Rome by Claudius. Saying 'Italy' instead of 'Rome' may well be another note of caution. We may smile at the suggestion (verse 22) that this letter is a 'quite brief' word of exhortation, and wonder what a long one would have looked like. On the other hand, when we compare the letter with some of the philosophical treatises written in the first two or three centuries of our era, it is indeed brief, and the writer has given one or two hints of places where he could have said much more.

The crowning glory of this final passage is the great blessing in verses 20 and 21, which is still used regularly in many churches, especially in the Easter season. The writer has not, up to this point, made much of the actual **resurrection** of Jesus, though he has assumed it throughout. He has chosen to concentrate more on his sacrificial death on the one hand, and his going on our behalf into the **heavenly** sanctuary on the other. But both of these only make the sense they do because Jesus was raised from the dead, as the whole New Testament insists on page after page. And here, in drawing together the lines of thought in the letter as a whole, this finally becomes explicit.

God 'led up' Jesus, back from the world of the dead, demonstrating that he was indeed 'the great shepherd of the sheep'. His blood, shed on the cross, has become the sacrificial blood which inaugurates the new **covenant**, the ultimate bond between God and his people, the agreement between them which brings in the '**age to come**' for which Israel had longed. That's what 'eternal' really means: not just 'going on for ever and ever' (which sometimes sounds a bit boring), but 'in relation to God's new age', in which there will be new tasks, new possibilities, new creative challenges.

Nor do we have to wait for 'life after death' for these to begin. God desires to accomplish them, at least in a preliminary way, through his people even in the present. That's why this blessing goes on to pray that God will 'put you into proper condition in every good work to do his will' (verse 21). When someone is getting ready to do a great task, they are trained up and kitted out for it, whether it's a lawyer getting ready to work in the courtroom, a plumber needing all the tools of the trade or, like my friend, a bishop getting ready to take on responsibility for part of God's church. Hebrews is praying that, whatever task each Christian is called to undertake, God will equip him or her fully for it, not only outwardly but also inwardly, so that he or she will 'perform', or accomplish, whatever will be pleasing in his sight.

Here we are at the heart of the mystery of Christian living, Christian leadership and Christian work for the **kingdom**. It is quite clear from the whole letter that to engage in such work requires effort, determination and patience. The fact that God is at work within us, as individuals and as communities, doesn't take that away. But, as we prepare for the work, engage in it and thank God for it when it's done, we must never forget that it is, ultimately, something that he does, mysteriously, in and through us.

Like Jesus himself, we may have to undergo great struggles as we learn what this means in practice (5.7–9). Indeed, if it really is 'through Jesus' that God is at work in us, we should expect that this will be the case. All the more reason, then, from start to finish, to give him 'glory for ever and ever'. He is the one who pioneered the way, who makes it possible for us to enter even now into God's very presence, and who waits to welcome us to the city that is to come. He is also the one through whom, because of his death, resurrection and ascension, and because of the gift of his own **spirit**, we are enabled to do and to be what we are called to do and to be, and to face the consequences with joy.

All this and more is summed up in the closing greeting: grace be with you.

GLOSSARY

age to come, *see* **present age**

apostle, disciple, the Twelve
'Apostle' means 'one who is sent'. It could be used of an ambassador or official delegate. In the New Testament it is sometimes used specifically of Jesus' inner circle of twelve; but Paul sees not only himself but several others outside the Twelve as 'apostles', the criterion being whether the person had personally seen the risen Jesus. Jesus' own choice of twelve close associates symbolized his plan to renew God's people, Israel; after the death of Judas Iscariot (Matthew 27.5; Acts 1.18) Matthias was chosen by lot to take his place, preserving the symbolic meaning. During Jesus' lifetime they, and many other followers, were seen as his 'disciples', which means 'pupils' or 'apprentices'.

baptism
Literally, 'plunging' people into water. From within a wider Jewish tradition of ritual washings and bathings, **John the Baptist** undertook a vocation of baptizing people in the Jordan, not as one ritual among others but as a unique moment of **repentance**, preparing them for the coming of the **kingdom of God.** Jesus himself was baptized by John, identifying himself with this renewal movement and developing it in his own way. His followers in turn baptized others. After his **resurrection**, and the sending of the **holy spirit**, baptism became the normal sign and means of entry into the community of Jesus' people. As early as Paul it was aligned both with the **Exodus** from Egypt (1 Corinthians 10.2) and with Jesus' death and resurrection (Romans 6.2–11).

circumcision, circumcised
The cutting off of the foreskin. Male circumcision was a major mark

of identity for Jews, following its initial commandment to Abraham (Genesis 17), reinforced by Joshua (Joshua 5.2–9). Other peoples, e.g. the Egyptians, also circumcised male children. A line of thought from Deuteronomy (e.g. 30.6), through Jeremiah (e.g. 31.33), to the **Dead Sea Scrolls** and the New Testament (e.g. Romans 2.29) speaks of 'circumcision of the heart' as God's real desire, by which one may become inwardly what the male Jew is outwardly, that is, marked out as part of God's people. At periods of Jewish assimilation into the surrounding culture, some Jews tried to remove the marks of circumcision (e.g. 1 Maccabees 1.11–15).

covenant

At the heart of Jewish belief is the conviction that the one God, YHWH, who had made the whole world, had called Abraham and his family to belong to him in a special way. The promises God made to Abraham and his family, and the requirements that were laid on them as a result, came to be seen in terms either of the agreement that a king would make with a subject people, or sometimes of the marriage bond between husband and wife. One regular way of describing this relationship was 'covenant', which can thus include both promise and **law**. The covenant was renewed at Mount Sinai with the giving of the **Torah**; in Deuteronomy before the entry to the promised land; and, in a more focused way, with David (e.g. Psalm 89). Jeremiah 31 promised that after the punishment of **exile** God would make a 'new covenant' with his people, forgiving them and binding them to him more intimately. Jesus believed that this was coming true through his **kingdom** proclamation and his death and **resurrection**. The early Christians developed these ideas in various ways, believing that in Jesus the promises had at last been fulfilled.

Dead Sea Scrolls

A collection of texts, some in remarkably good repair, some extremely fragmentary, found in the late 1940s around Qumran (near the northeast corner of the Dead Sea), and virtually all now edited, translated and in the public domain. They formed all or part of the library of a strict monastic group, most likely Essenes, founded in the mid-second century BC and lasting until the Jewish–Roman war of 66–70. The scrolls include the earliest existing manuscripts of the Hebrew and Aramaic scriptures, and several other important documents of community regulations, scriptural exegesis, hymns, wisdom writings, and other literature. They shed a flood of light on one small segment within the Judaism of Jesus' day, helping us to understand how some Jews at least were thinking, praying and reading scripture. Despite attempts to prove the contrary, they make no reference to **John the Baptist**, Jesus, Paul, James or early Christianity in general.

demons, *see* **the satan**

devil, *see* **the satan**

Essenes, *see* **Dead Sea Scrolls**

eternal life, *see* **present age**

eucharist

The meal in which the earliest Christians, and Christians ever since, obeyed Jesus' command to 'do this in remembrance of him' at the Last Supper (Luke 22.19; 1 Corinthians 11.23–26). The word 'eucharist' itself comes from the Greek for 'thanksgiving'; it means, basically, 'the thank-you meal', and looks back to the many times when Jesus took bread, gave thanks for it, broke it, and gave it to people (e.g. Luke 24.30; John 6.11). Other early phrases for the same meal are 'the Lord's supper' (1 Corinthians 11.20) and 'the breaking of bread' (Acts 2.42). Later it came to be called 'the Mass' (from the Latin word at the end of the service, meaning 'sent out') and 'Holy Communion' (Paul speaks of 'sharing' or 'communion' in the body and blood of Christ). Later theological controversies about the precise meaning of the various actions and elements of the meal should not obscure its centrality in earliest Christian living and its continuing vital importance today.

exile

Deuteronomy (29—30) warned that if Israel disobeyed YHWH, he would send his people into exile, but that if they then repented he would bring them back. When the Babylonians sacked Jerusalem and took the people into exile, prophets such as Jeremiah interpreted this as the fulfilment of this prophecy, and made further promises about how long exile would last (70 years, according to Jeremiah 25.12; 29.10). Sure enough, exiles began to return in the late sixth century (Ezra 1.1). However, the post-exilic period was largely a disappointment, since the people were still enslaved to foreigners (Nehemiah 9.36); and at the height of persecution by the Syrians, Daniel 9.2, 24 spoke of the 'real' exile lasting not for 70 years but for 70 *weeks* of years, i.e., 490 years. Longing for the real 'return from exile', when the prophecies of Isaiah, Jeremiah, etc. would be fulfilled, and redemption from pagan oppression accomplished, continued to characterize many Jewish movements, and was a major theme in Jesus' proclamation and his summons to **repentance**.

Exodus

The Exodus from Egypt took place, according to the book of that name, under the leadership of Moses, after long years in which the Israelites had been enslaved there. (According to Genesis 15.13f., this was itself part of God's covenanted promise to Abraham.) It demonstrated, to them and to Pharaoh, King of Egypt, that Israel was God's special child (Exodus 4.22). They then wandered through the Sinai wilderness for 40 years, led by God in a pillar of cloud and fire; early on in this time they were given the **Torah** on Mount Sinai itself. Finally, after the death of Moses and under the leadership of Joshua, they crossed the Jordan and entered, and eventually conquered, the promised land of Canaan. This event, commemorated annually in Passover and other Jewish festivals, gave the Israelites not only a powerful memory of what had made them a people, but also a particular shape and content to their faith in YHWH as not only creator but also redeemer; and in subsequent enslavements, particularly the **exile**, they looked for a further redemption which would be, in effect, a new Exodus. Probably no other past event so dominated the imagination of first-century Jews; among them the early Christians, following the lead of Jesus himself, continually referred back to the Exodus to give meaning and shape to their own critical events, most particularly Jesus' death and **resurrection**.

faith

Faith in the New Testament covers a wide area of human trust and trustworthiness, merging into love at one end of the scale and loyalty at the other. Within Jewish and Christian thinking faith in God also includes *belief*, accepting certain things as true about God, and what he has done in the world (e.g. bringing Israel out of Egypt; raising Jesus from the dead). For Jesus, 'faith' often seems to mean 'recognizing that God is decisively at work to bring the **kingdom** through Jesus'. For Paul, 'faith' is both the specific belief that Jesus is Lord and that God raised him from the dead (Romans 10.9) and the response of grateful human love to sovereign divine love (Galatians 2.20). This faith is, for Paul, the solitary badge of membership in God's people in **Christ**, marking them out in a way that **Torah**, and the works it prescribes, can never do.

Gentiles

The Jews divided the world into Jews and non-Jews. The Hebrew word for non-Jews, *goyim*, carries overtones both of family identity (i.e., not of Jewish ancestry) and of worship (i.e. of idols, not of the one true God YHWH). Though many Jews established good relations with Gentiles, not least in the Jewish Diaspora (the dispersion of Jews away from Palestine), officially there were taboos against contact such as intermarriage. In the New Testament the Greek word *ethne*, 'nations', carries the same meanings as *goyim*. Part of Paul's overmastering agenda was to insist that Gentiles who believed in Jesus had full rights in the Christian community alongside believing Jews, without having to become **circumcised**.

good news, gospel, message, word

The idea of 'good news', for which an older English word is 'gospel', had two principal meanings for first-century Jews. First, with roots in Isaiah, it meant the news of YHWH's long-awaited victory over evil and rescue of his people. Second, it was used in the Roman world of the accession, or birthday, or the emperor. Since for Jesus and Paul the announcement of God's inbreaking **kingdom** was both the fulfilment of prophecy and a challenge to the world's present rulers, 'gospel' became an important shorthand for both the message of Jesus himself, and the apostolic message about him. Paul saw this message as itself the vehicle of God's saving power (Romans 1.16; 1 Thessalonians 2.13).

The four canonical 'gospels' tell the story of Jesus in such a way as to bring out both these aspects (unlike some other so-called 'gospels' circulated in the second and subsequent centuries, which tended both to cut off the scriptural and Jewish roots of Jesus' achievement and to inculcate a private spirituality rather than confrontation with the world's rulers). Since in Isaiah this creative, life-giving good news was seen as God's own powerful word (40.8; 55.11), the early Christians could use 'word' or 'message' as another shorthand for the basic Christian proclamation.

gospel, *see* **good news**

heaven

Heaven is God's dimension of the created order (Genesis 1.1; Psalm 115.16; Matthew 6.9), whereas 'earth' is the world of space, time and matter that we know. 'Heaven' thus sometimes stands, reverentially, for 'God' (as in Matthew's regular '**kingdom** of heaven'). Normally hidden from human sight, heaven is occasionally revealed or unveiled so that people can see God's dimension of ordinary life (e.g. 2 Kings 6.17; Revelation 1, 4—5). Heaven in the New Testament is thus not usually seen as the place where God's people go after death; at the end the New Jerusalem descends *from* heaven *to* earth, joining the two dimensions for ever. 'Entering the kingdom of heaven' does not mean 'going to heaven after death', but belonging in the present to the people who steer their earthly course by the standards and purposes of heaven (cf. the Lord's Prayer: 'on earth as in heaven', Matthew 6. 10) and who are assured of membership in the **age to come.**

high priest, *see* **priests**

holy spirit

In Genesis 1.2, the spirit is God's presence and power *within* creation, without God being identified with creation. The same spirit entered people, notably the prophets, enabling them to speak and act for God. At his **baptism** by **John the Baptist**, Jesus was specially equipped with the spirit, resulting in his remarkable public career (Acts 10.38). After

his **resurrection**, his followers were themselves filled (Acts 2) by the
same spirit, now identified as Jesus' own spirit: the creator God was
acting afresh, remaking the world and them too. The spirit enabled
them to live out a holiness which the **Torah** could not, producing
'fruit' in their lives, giving them 'gifts' with which to serve God, the
world, and the church, and assuring them of future resurrection
(Romans 8; Galatians 4—5; 1 Corinthians 12—14). From very early in
Christianity (e.g. Galatians 4.1–7), the spirit became part of the new
revolutionary definition of God himself: 'the one who sends the son
and the spirit of the son'.

John (the Baptist)

Jesus' cousin on his mother's side, born a few months before Jesus; his
father was a **priest**. He acted as a prophet, baptizing in the Jordan –
dramatically re-enacting the **Exodus** from Egypt – to prepare people,
by **repentance**, for God's coming judgment. He may have had some
contact with the **Essenes**, though his eventual public message was different from theirs. Jesus' own vocation was decisively confirmed at his
baptism by John. As part of John's message of the **kingdom**, he out-
spokenly criticized Herod Antipas for marrying his brother's wife.
Herod had him imprisoned, and then beheaded him at his wife's
request (Mark 6.14–29). Groups of John's disciples continued a separate
existence, without merging into Christianity, for some time afterwards
(e.g. Acts 19.1–7).

justification

God's declaration, from his position as judge of all the world, that
someone is in the right, despite universal sin. This declaration will be
made on the last day on the basis of an entire life (Romans 2.1–16),
but is brought forward into the present on the basis of Jesus' achievement, because sin has been dealt with through his cross (Romans
3.21—4.25); the means of this present justification is simply **faith**.
This means, particularly, that Jews and **Gentiles** alike are full members
of the family promised by God to Abraham (Galatians 3; Romans 4).

kingdom of God, kingdom of heaven

Best understood as the king*ship*, or sovereign and saving rule, of Israel's
God YHWH, as celebrated in several psalms (e.g. 99.1) and prophecies

(e.g. Daniel 6.26f.). Because YHWH was the creator God, when he finally became king in the way he intended this would involve setting the world to rights, and particularly rescuing Israel from its enemies. 'Kingdom of God' and various equivalents (e.g. 'No king but God!') became a revolutionary slogan around the time of Jesus. Jesus' own announcement of God's kingdom redefined these expectations around his own very different plan and vocation. His invitation to people to 'enter' the kingdom was a way of summoning them to allegiance to himself and his programme, seen as the start of God's long-awaited saving reign. For Jesus, the kingdom was coming not in a single move, but in stages, of which his own public career was one, his death and **resurrection** another, and a still future consummation another. Note that 'kingdom of **heaven**' is Matthew's preferred form for the same phrase, following a regular Jewish practice of saying 'heaven' rather than 'God'. It does not refer to a place ('heaven'), but to the fact of God's becoming king in and through Jesus and his achievement. Paul speaks of Jesus, as **Messiah**, already in possession of his kingdom, waiting to hand it over finally to the father (1 Corinthians 15.23–28; cf. Ephesians 5.5).

law, *see* **Torah**

life, soul, spirit
Ancient people held many different views about what made human beings the special creatures they are. Some, including many Jews, believed that to be complete, humans needed bodies as well as inner selves. Others, including many influenced by the philosophy of Plato (fourth century BC), believed that the important part of a human was the 'soul' (Gk: *psyche*), which at death would be happily freed from its bodily prison. Confusingly for us, the same word *psyche* is often used in the New Testament within a Jewish framework where it clearly means 'life' or 'true self', without implying a body/soul dualism that devalues the body. Human inwardness of experience and understanding can also be referred to as 'spirit'. *See also* **resurrection**.

message, *see* **good news**

Messiah, messianic, Christ

The Hebrew word means literally 'anointed one', hence in theory either a prophet, **priest** or king. In Greek this translates as *Christos*; 'Christ' in early Christianity was a title, and only gradually became an alternative proper name for Jesus. In practice 'Messiah' is mostly restricted to the notion, which took various forms in ancient Judaism, of the coming king who would be David's true heir, through whom YHWH would bring judgment to the world, and in particular would rescue Israel from pagan enemies. There was no single template of expectations. Scriptural stories and promises contributed to different ideals and movements, often focused on (a) decisive military defeat of Israel's enemies and (b) rebuilding or cleansing the **Temple**. The **Dead Sea Scrolls** speak of two 'Messiahs', one a priest and the other a king. The universal early Christian belief that Jesus was Messiah is only explicable, granted his crucifixion by the Romans (which would have been seen as a clear sign that he was not the Messiah), by their belief that God had raised him from the dead, so vindicating the implicit messianic claims of his earlier ministry.

Mishnah

The main codification of Jewish law (**Torah**) by the **rabbis**, produced in about AD 200, reducing to writing the 'oral Torah' which in Jesus' day ran parallel to the 'written Torah'. The Mishnah is itself the basis of the much larger collections of traditions in the two Talmuds (roughly AD 400).

parables

From the Old Testament onwards, prophets and other teachers used various storytelling devices as vehicles for their challenge to Israel (e.g. 2 Samuel 12.1–7). Sometimes these appeared as visions with interpretations (e.g. Daniel 7). Similar techniques were used by the **rabbis**. Jesus made his own creative adaptation of these traditions, in order to break open the world-view of his contemporaries and to invite them to share his vision of God's **kingdom** instead. His stories portrayed this as something that was *happening*, not just a timeless truth, and enabled his hearers to step inside the story and make it their own. As with some Old Testament visions, some of Jesus' parables have their own interpretations (e.g. the sower, Mark 4); others are thinly disguised retellings of the prophetic story of Israel (e.g. the wicked tenants, Mark 12).

Pharisees, legal experts, lawyers, rabbis

The Pharisees were an unofficial but powerful Jewish pressure group through most of the first centuries BC and AD. Largely lay-led, though including some **priests**, their aim was to purify Israel through intensified observance of the Jewish law (**Torah**), developing their own traditions about the precise meaning and application of scripture, their own patterns of prayer and other devotion, and their own calculations of the national hope. Though not all legal experts were Pharisees, most Pharisees were thus legal experts.

They effected a democratization of Israel's life, since for them the study and practice of Torah was equivalent to worshipping in the **Temple** – though they were adamant in pressing their own rules for the Temple liturgy on an unwilling (and often **Sadducean**) priesthood. This enabled them to survive AD 70 and, merging into the early rabbinic movement, to develop new ways forward. Politically they stood up for ancestral traditions, and were at the forefront of various movements of revolt against both pagan overlordship and compromised Jewish leaders. By Jesus' day there were two distinct schools, the stricter one of Shammai, more inclined towards armed revolt, and the more lenient one of Hillel, ready to live and let live.

Jesus' debates with the Pharisees are at least as much a matter of agenda and policy (Jesus strongly opposed their separatist nationalism) as about details of theology and piety. Saul of Tarsus was a fervent right-wing Pharisee, presumably a Shammaite, until his conversion.

After the disastrous war of AD 66–70, these schools of Hillel and Shammai continued bitter debate on appropriate policy. Following the further disaster of AD 135 (the failed Bar-Kochba revolt against Rome) their traditions were carried on by the rabbis who, though looking to the earlier Pharisees for inspiration, developed a Torah-piety in which personal holiness and purity took the place of political agendas.

present age, age to come, eternal life

By the time of Jesus many Jewish thinkers divided history into two periods: 'the present age' and 'the age to come' – the latter being the time when YHWH would at last act decisively to judge evil, to rescue Israel, and to create a new world of justice and peace. The early Christians believed that, though the full blessings of the coming age lay still in the future, it had already begun with Jesus, particularly with his death and **resurrection**, and that by **faith** and **baptism** they were able to enter it already. 'Eternal life' does not mean simply 'existence continuing without end', but 'the life of the age to come'.

priests, high priest

Aaron, the older brother of Moses, was appointed Israel's first high priest (Exodus 28—29), and in theory his descendants were Israel's priests thereafter. Other members of his tribe (Levi) were 'Levites', performing other liturgical duties but not sacrificing. Priests lived among the people all around the country, having a local teaching role (Leviticus 10.11; Malachi 2.7), and going to Jerusalem by rotation to perform the **Temple** liturgy (e.g. Luke 2.8).

David appointed Zadok (whose Aaronic ancestry is sometimes questioned) as high priest, and his family remained thereafter the senior priests in Jerusalem, probably the ancestors of the **Sadducees**. One explanation of the origins of the **Qumran** Essenes is that they were a dissident group who believed themselves to be the rightful chief priests.

Qumran, *see* Dead Sea Scrolls

rabbis, *see* Pharisees

repentance

Literally, this means 'turning back'. It is widely used in the Old Testament and subsequent Jewish literature to indicate both a personal turning away from sin and Israel's corporate turning away from idolatry and back to YHWH. Through both meanings, it is linked to the idea of 'return from **exile**'; if Israel is to 'return' in all senses, it must 'return' to YHWH. This is at the heart of the summons of both **John the Baptist** and Jesus. In Paul's writings it is mostly used for **Gentiles** turning away from idols to serve the true God; also for sinning Christians who need to return to Jesus.

resurrection

In most biblical thought, human bodies matter and are not merely disposable prisons for the **soul**. When ancient Israelites wrestled with the goodness and justice of YHWH, the creator, they ultimately came to insist that he must raise the dead (Isaiah 26.19; Daniel 12.2–3) – a suggestion firmly resisted by classical pagan thought. The longed-for return from **exile** was also spoken of in terms of YHWH raising dry bones to new **life** (Ezekiel 37.1–14). These ideas were developed in the second-**Temple** period, not least at times of martyrdom (e.g. 2 Maccabees 7). Resurrection was not just 'life after death', but a newly embodied life *after* 'life after death'; those at present dead were either 'asleep', or seen as 'souls', 'angels' or 'spirits', awaiting new embodiment.

The early Christian belief that Jesus had been raised from the dead was not that he had 'gone to **heaven**', or that he had been 'exalted', or was 'divine'; they believed all those as well, but each could have been expressed without mention of resurrection. Only the bodily resurrection of Jesus explains the rise of the early church, particularly its belief in Jesus' messiahship (which his crucifixion would have called into question). The early Christians believed that they themselves would be raised to a new, transformed bodily life at the time of the Lord's return or **parousia** (e.g. Philippians 3.20f.).

sabbath

The Jewish sabbath, the seventh day of the week, was a regular reminder both of creation (Genesis 2.3; Exodus 20.8–11) and of the **Exodus** (Deuteronomy 5.15). Along with **circumcision** and the food laws, it was one of the badges of Jewish identity within the pagan world of late antiquity, and a considerable body of Jewish **law** and custom grew up around its observance.

sacrifice

Like all ancient people, the Israelites offered animal and vegetable sacrifices to their God. Unlike others, they possessed a highly detailed written code (mostly in Leviticus) for what to offer and how to offer it; this in turn was developed in the **Mishnah** (*c*. AD 200). The Old Testament specifies that sacrifices can only be offered in the Jerusalem **Temple**; after this was destroyed in AD 70, sacrifices ceased, and

Judaism developed further the idea, already present in some teachings, of prayer, fasting and almsgiving as alternative forms of sacrifice. The early Christians used the language of sacrifice in connection with such things as holiness, evangelism and the **eucharist**.

Sadducees

By Jesus' day, the Sadducees were the aristocracy of Judaism, possibly tracing their origins to the family of Zadok, David's **high priest**. Based in Jerusalem, and including most of the leading priestly families, they had their own traditions and attempted to resist the pressure of the **Pharisees** to conform to theirs. They claimed to rely only on the Pentateuch (the first five books of the Old Testament), and denied any doctrine of a future life, particularly of the **resurrection** and other ideas associated with it, presumably because of the encouragement such beliefs gave to revolutionary movements. No writings from the Sadducees have survived, unless the apocryphal book of Ben-Sirach ('Ecclesiasticus') comes from them. The Sadducees themselves did not survive the destruction of Jerusalem and the **Temple** in AD 70.

the satan, 'the accuser', demons

The Bible is never very precise about the identity of the figure known as 'the satan'. The Hebrew word means 'the accuser', and at times the satan seems to be a member of YHWH's heavenly council, with special responsibility as director of prosecutions (1 Chronicles 21.1; Job 1—2; Zechariah 3.1f.). However, it becomes identified variously with the serpent of the garden of Eden (Genesis 3.1–15) and with the rebellious daystar cast out of **heaven** (Isaiah 14.12–15), and was seen by many Jews as the quasi-personal source of evil standing behind both human wickedness and large-scale injustice, sometimes operating through semi-independent 'demons'. By Jesus' time various words were used to denote this figure, including Beelzebul/b (lit. 'Lord of the flies') and simply 'the evil one'; Jesus warned his followers against the deceits this figure could perpetrate. His opponents accused him of being in league with the satan, but the early Christians believed that Jesus in fact defeated it both in his own struggles with temptation (Matthew 4; Luke 4), his exorcisms of demons, and his death (1 Corinthians 2.8; Colossians 2.15). Final victory over this ultimate enemy is thus assured

(Revelation 20), though the struggle can still be fierce for Christians (Ephesians 6.10–20).

son of David, David's son

An alternative, and infrequently used, title for **Messiah**. The messianic promises of the Old Testament often focus specifically on David's son, for example 2 Samuel 7.12–16; Psalm 89.19–37. Joseph, Mary's husband, is called 'son of David' by the angel in Matthew 1.20.

son of God

Originally a title for Israel (Exodus 4.22) and the Davidic king (Psalm 2.7); also used of ancient angelic figures (Genesis 6.2). By the New Testament period it was already used as a **messianic** title, for example in the **Dead Sea Scrolls**. There, and when used of Jesus in the **gospels** (e.g. Matthew 16.16), it means, or reinforces, 'Messiah', without the later significance of 'divine'. However, already in Paul the transition to the fuller meaning (one who was already equal with God and was sent by him to become human and to become Messiah) is apparent, without loss of the meaning 'Messiah' itself (e.g. Galatians 4.4).

son of man

In Hebrew or Aramaic, this simply means 'mortal' or 'human being'; in later Judaism, it is sometimes used to mean 'I' or 'someone like me'. In the New Testament the phrase is frequently linked to Daniel 7.13, where 'one like a son of man' is brought on the clouds of **heaven** to 'the Ancient of Days', being vindicated after a period of suffering, and is given kingly power. Though Daniel 7 itself interprets this as code for 'the people of the saints of the Most High', by the first century some Jews understood it as a **messianic** promise. Jesus developed this in his own way in certain key sayings which are best understood as promises that God would vindicate him, and judge those who had opposed him, after his own suffering (e.g. Mark 14.62). Jesus was thus able to use the phrase as a cryptic self-designation, hinting at his coming suffering, his vindication and his God-given authority.

soul, *see* life

spirit, *see* **life, holy spirit**

Temple

The Temple in Jerusalem was planned by David (*c.* 1000 BC) and built by his son Solomon as the central sanctuary for all Israel. After reforms under Hezekiah and Josiah in the seventh century BC, it was destroyed by Babylon in 587 BC. Rebuilding by the returned **exiles** began in 538 BC, and was completed in 516, initiating the 'second Temple period'. Judas Maccabaeus cleansed it in 164 BC after its desecration by Antiochus Epiphanes (167). Herod the Great began to rebuild and beautify it in 19 BC; the work was completed in AD 63. The Temple was destroyed by the Romans in AD 70. Many Jews believed it should and would be rebuilt; some still do. The Temple was not only the place of **sacrifice**; it was believed to be the unique dwelling of YHWH on earth, the place where **heaven** and earth met.

Torah, Jewish law

'Torah', narrowly conceived, consists of the first five books of the Old Testament, the 'five books of Moses' or 'Pentateuch'. (These contain much law, but also much narrative.) It can also be used for the whole Old Testament scriptures, though strictly these are the 'law, prophets and writings'. In a broader sense, it refers to the whole developing corpus of Jewish legal tradition, written and oral; the oral Torah was initially codified in the **Mishnah** around AD 200, with wider developments found in the two Talmuds, of Babylon and Jerusalem, codified around AD 400. Many Jews in the time of Jesus and Paul regarded the Torah as being so strongly God-given as to be almost itself, in some sense, divine; some (e.g. Ben Sirach 24) identified it with the figure of 'Wisdom'. Doing what Torah said was not seen as a means of earning God's favour, but rather of expressing gratitude, and as a key badge of Jewish identity.

word, *see* **good news**

Word

The prologue to John's gospel (1.1–18) uses Word (Greek: *logos*) in a special sense, based on the ancient Israelite view of God's Word in creation and new creation. Here the Word is Jesus, the personal presence of the God who remains other than the world. He is the one through whom creation came into being; he is the one, now, through whom it will be healed and restored.

YHWH

The ancient Israelite name for God, from at least the time of the **Exodus** (Exodus 6.2f.). It may originally have been pronounced 'Yahweh', but by the time of Jesus it was considered too holy to speak out loud, except for the **high priest** once a year in the Holy of Holies in the **Temple**. Instead, when reading scripture, pious Jews would say *Adonai*, 'Lord', marking this usage by adding the vowels of *Adonai* to the consonants of YHWH, eventually producing the hybrid 'Jehovah'. The word YHWH is formed from the verb 'to be', combining 'I am who I am', 'I will be who I will be', and perhaps 'I am because I am', emphasizing YHWH's sovereign creative power.